EXPLORE COLOMBIA

CHARLES BWENA

DEDICATION

To all travelers seeking adventure, culture, and unforgettable experiences. May this guide book inspire you to explore the vibrant and diverse country of Colombia and discover its hidden treasures. Safe travels and happy exploring!

TABLE OF CONTENT

INTRODUCTION

Purpose of the guide book

My name is Charles, and I have always been passionate about travel. Over the years, I have visited many countries around the world, each with its own unique culture, history, and beauty. But no matter where I go, I always find myself coming back to Colombia.

As a Colombian-American, I have a special connection to this country. I grew up hearing stories of my parents' homeland - of its lush rainforests, colorful festivals, and warm, welcoming people. When I finally had the chance to visit Colombia for myself, I was blown away by all that it had to offer. From the vibrant cities to the remote mountain villages, every corner of this country seemed to hold a new adventure.

But as much as I loved Colombia, I also knew that it could be a challenging place to travel, especially for those who are unfamiliar with its customs and traditions. That's why I decided to write this guidebook - to provide practical advice and tips for travelers who are planning a trip to Colombia.

Through my personal experiences and insights, I hope to help travelers navigate the country's unique challenges and make the most of their time here. I want to offer advice on everything from transportation and safety to cultural norms and etiquette. I also want to showcase the incredible diversity and beauty of Colombia, from its bustling cities to its pristine beaches and cloud forests.

But more than that, I want to encourage travelers to approach Colombia with an open mind and an open heart. This is a country that has faced many challenges over the years, but it is also a country of great resilience, creativity, and warmth. I hope that this guidebook will help travelers to connect with the people and cultures of Colombia in a meaningful way, and to leave with a deep appreciation for all that this country has to offer.

Whether you are a first-time traveler or a seasoned adventurer, I invite you to join me on a journey through the vibrant and enchanting landscapes of Colombia.

Benefits of preparation

There are many benefits to preparing thoroughly before embarking on a trip to Colombia. Here are just a few:

1. Enhanced safety: Colombia has made significant progress in recent years in terms of improving security and reducing violence. However, as with any country, there are still certain areas that can be dangerous for travelers. By doing your research and planning ahead, you can identify any potential risks and take steps to avoid them. You can also learn about common scams and safety tips to help you stay safe while traveling.

2. Better understanding of the culture: Colombia is a diverse and complex country, with many different cultures and traditions. By learning about these customs ahead of time, you can better understand and appreciate the people and places you encounter on your trip. You can also avoid unintentionally offending anyone by being aware of cultural norms and etiquette.

3. More efficient use of time: Colombia is a large country with many different regions and attractions to explore. By planning your itinerary ahead of time, you can make the most of your time and ensure that you don't miss out on any must-see sights or experiences. You can also book tickets and accommodations in advance to save time and money.

4. Greater sense of confidence: Traveling to a new country can be intimidating, especially if you don't speak the language or are unfamiliar with the customs. By preparing well in advance, you can approach your trip with a greater sense of confidence and ease. You'll also be better equipped to handle any unexpected challenges or situations that may arise.

5. More meaningful experiences: Finally, by preparing thoroughly for your trip to Colombia, you can have more meaningful and enriching experiences. You'll be able to connect more deeply with the people and cultures you encounter, and you'll have a greater appreciation for

the country's history, traditions, and natural beauty. Ultimately, this can lead to a more fulfilling and memorable travel experience.

How to use the guide book

This guidebook is designed to be a comprehensive resource for anyone planning a trip to Colombia. Here are some tips on how to use it effectively:

1. Read through the introduction: The introductory section of this guidebook provides important context and background information on Colombia. It also includes a personal story that illustrates the purpose of the guidebook. Take the time to read through this section to gain a deeper understanding of the country and the goals of the guidebook.

2. Use the table of contents: The table of contents provides a detailed overview of the topics covered in the guidebook. Use it to quickly locate the information you need and to navigate to specific sections of the book.

3. Focus on the sections that are most relevant to your trip: Depending on the nature of your trip to Colombia, some sections of the guidebook may be more useful to you than others. For example, if you are planning a backpacking trip, you may want to focus on the sections on transportation, accommodation, and budgeting. If you are interested in cultural experiences, you may want to focus on the sections on history, festivals, and food.

4. Take notes and highlight key information: As you read through the guidebook, take notes on important information such as contact details for accommodations, transportation options, and must-see attractions. You may also want to highlight key tips and advice that are particularly relevant to your trip.

5. Refer back to the guidebook during your trip: This guidebook is designed to be a practical resource that you can refer back to during your trip. Keep a copy with you as you travel and use it to help you navigate new experiences and challenges.

By following these tips, you can use this guidebook to plan and enjoy a safe, fulfilling, and memorable trip to Colombia.

CHAPTER ONE

DESTINATION SELECTION

Factors to consider when choosing a destination
Choosing a travel destination is an exciting and challenging process. There are countless amazing places to explore around the world, each with its own unique culture, attractions, and experiences to offer. However, with so many options to choose from, it can be difficult to know where to start. In this chapter, we will explore some of the key factors to consider when choosing a travel destination.

1. Budget One of the most important factors to consider when choosing a travel destination is your budget. The cost of travel can vary widely depending on the destination, time of year, and type of accommodation and activities you choose. Before you start researching potential destinations, it's important to have a clear idea of your budget and what you can afford to spend on your trip. This will help you narrow down your options and focus on destinations that are within your price range.

2. Time of year the time of year can have a significant impact on your travel experience, so it's important to consider the climate and weather patterns of your potential destinations. For example, if you are looking for a tropical beach vacation, you may want to avoid destinations that are prone to hurricanes or monsoons during the time of year you are planning to travel. On the other hand, if you are interested in winter sports like skiing or snowboarding, you'll want to choose a destination that has reliable snowfall during your trip.

3. Interests and preferences When choosing a travel destination, it's important to consider your interests and preferences. Do you prefer urban or rural environments? Are you interested in history, art, or nature? Do you prefer adventurous or more relaxing activities? The answers to these questions can help guide you towards destinations that are a good fit for your personal preferences and interests.

4. Accessibility and logistics Accessibility and logistics are also important factors to consider when choosing a travel destination. How easy is it to get to your destination? Are there direct flights, or will you need to make connections? How long is the travel time? Once you arrive, how easy is it to get around the destination? Are there public transportation options or will you need to rent a car? These logistical considerations can have a significant impact on your travel experience, so it's important to research them carefully.

5. Safety and security Safety and security are always important considerations when traveling, but they have become even more important in recent years due to global security concerns. Before choosing a travel destination, it's important to research the safety and security situation in the country or region you are considering. This can include looking at travel advisories issued by your government, reading news articles and blogs, and talking to other travelers who have visited the destination.

6. Culture and language the culture and language of your potential destinations can also have a significant impact on your travel experience. It's important to research the local customs and etiquette, as well as any language barriers that may exist. Will you need to learn some basic phrases in the local language to get by, or is English widely spoken? Are there cultural practices or traditions that you should be aware of before visiting? Understanding the local culture can help you navigate new experiences and connect more deeply with the local people.

7. Personal goals and aspirations Finally, when choosing a travel destination, it's important to consider your personal goals and aspirations. What do you hope to gain from your travel experience? Are you looking for adventure, relaxation, or cultural immersion? Do you want to challenge yourself, learn new skills, or simply have fun? By understanding your personal goals and aspirations, you can choose a travel destination that is a good fit for your unique needs and desires.

8. In conclusion, choosing a travel destination is a complex process that involves a wide range of factors. By considering your budget, the time of year, your interests and preferences

Popular destinations and their features

Colombia is a diverse and beautiful country, with a wide range of destinations that offer something for every type of traveler. From vibrant cities to stunning natural landscapes, there are countless amazing places to explore in Colombia. Here, we will highlight some of the most popular destinations in Colombia and their unique features.

1. Cartagena Cartagena is a historic city located on Colombia's Caribbean coast. It is known for its well-preserved colonial architecture, colorful streets, and vibrant cultural scene. Visitors to Cartagena can explore the city's historic center, which is surrounded by a massive stone wall built by the Spanish in the 16th century. The city is also home to numerous museums, art galleries, and cultural events, making it a great destination for history and culture enthusiasts. Cartagena is also a popular destination for beach lovers, with several nearby beaches that offer clear water and soft sand.

2. Medellin Medellin is a bustling city located in the heart of Colombia's Andean region. It is known for its innovative urban design, which includes a network of cable cars and escalators that connect the city's hillside neighborhoods to the downtown area. Visitors to Medellin can explore the city's museums, parks, and botanical gardens, as well as its vibrant nightlife and culinary scene. Medellin is also a great destination for outdoor enthusiasts, with several nearby national parks and nature reserves that offer hiking, birdwatching, and other outdoor activities.

3. Bogota Bogota is the capital city of Colombia and a cultural hub of the country. It is known for its rich history and architecture, including the historic La Candelaria neighborhood and the stunning Teatro Colon. Visitors to Bogota can explore the city's numerous museums and art galleries, as well as its lively street art scene. The city is also a great

destination for foodies, with a wide range of culinary options that reflect Colombia's diverse cultural influences.

4. Tayrona National Park Tayrona National Park is a stunning natural destination located on Colombia's Caribbean coast. It is known for its pristine beaches, crystal-clear water, and lush rainforests. Visitors to Tayrona can explore the park's numerous hiking trails, which lead through dense jungle and along scenic coastlines. The park is also home to several indigenous communities, offering visitors a chance to learn about the local culture and way of life.

5. San Andres and Providencia Islands San Andres and Providencia are two stunning Caribbean islands located off the coast of Colombia. They are known for their pristine beaches, clear water, and vibrant marine life. Visitors to San Andres and Providencia can enjoy snorkeling, scuba diving, and other water sports, as well as exploring the islands' unique cultural heritage. The islands are also a great destination for relaxation, with plenty of opportunities to soak up the sun and enjoy the laid-back island lifestyle.

6. The Coffee Region Colombia's Coffee Region is a beautiful and tranquil destination located in the heart of the country. It is known for its lush green hills, fertile valleys, and picturesque coffee plantations. Visitors to the Coffee Region can explore the region's charming towns and villages, learn about the process of coffee production, and enjoy the natural beauty of the area. The region is also a great destination for outdoor enthusiasts, with several nearby national parks and nature reserves that offer hiking, birdwatching, and other outdoor activities.

In conclusion, Colombia is a beautiful and diverse country with a wide range of popular destinations to explore. Whether you are interested in history and culture, natural beauty, outdoor adventure, or relaxation, there is something for everyone in Colombia. From the vibrant cities of Cartagena and Bogota to the stunning natural landscapes of Tayron

Travel trends and emerging destinations

As the world becomes more interconnected and accessible, travel trends continue to evolve, with new destinations and experiences emerging every year. Here, we will explore some of the latest travel trends and emerging destinations that are gaining popularity among travelers.

1. Sustainable Travel Sustainable travel has become an increasingly popular trend in recent years, as travelers seek to minimize their impact on the environment and support local communities. This can involve choosing eco-friendly accommodations, eating locally-sourced food, and participating in responsible tourism activities that benefit the local environment and culture. Many destinations around the world have embraced sustainable travel, offering eco-tourism experiences that prioritize environmental conservation and community development.

2. Wellness Travel Wellness travel is another growing trend, as travelers seek to prioritize their physical and mental health while on vacation. This can involve activities like yoga and meditation retreats, spa treatments, and outdoor activities like hiking and biking. Many destinations around the world have developed wellness tourism offerings, with a range of accommodations and activities that cater to the wellness traveler.

3. Digital Detox Travel With the rise of technology and social media, many travelers are seeking ways to disconnect and take a break from their devices. Digital detox travel involves unplugging from technology and focusing on experiencing the world in a more present and mindful way. This can involve activities like meditation, yoga, and nature walks, as well as staying in accommodations that don't have Wi-Fi or TV.

4. Emerging Destinations As popular destinations become more crowded and expensive, many travelers are seeking out emerging destinations that offer unique experiences and are less well-known. Some of the emerging destinations that are gaining popularity among travelers include:

- Georgia: This country in the Caucasus region of Europe is known for its stunning natural beauty, rich history, and delicious cuisine.

- Oman: This Middle Eastern country is a hidden gem, with stunning desert landscapes, beautiful beaches, and a rich cultural heritage.

- Rwanda: This African country is home to some of the world's last remaining mountain gorillas, as well as stunning national parks and a vibrant cultural scene.

- Uzbekistan: This Central Asian country is known for its beautiful mosques and mausoleums, as well as its rich history and culture.

5. Adventure Travel Adventure travel is a trend that continues to grow in popularity, as travelers seek out new and exciting experiences that push their limits. This can involve activities like trekking, white water rafting, and rock climbing, as well as exploring remote destinations that are off the beaten path. Many destinations around the world have developed adventure tourism offerings, with a range of activities and accommodations that cater to the adventurous traveler.

In conclusion, travel trends continue to evolve, with new destinations and experiences emerging every year. Whether you are interested in sustainable travel, wellness travel, digital detox travel, or adventure travel, there are countless destinations around the world that offer unique and exciting experiences for every type of traveler. By staying up-to-date on the latest travel trends and exploring emerging destinations, you can discover new and exciting ways to experience the world.

Travel Documents and Planning

Passport and visa requirements
If you are planning to visit Colombia, it is important to be aware of the passport and visa requirements for your travel. Here's what you need to know:

Passports:

To enter Colombia, you must have a valid passport. Your passport must be valid for at least six months beyond your planned departure date from Colombia. It is also recommended to have at least two blank pages in your passport for entry stamps.

Visas:

Most visitors to Colombia do not require a visa if their stay is less than 90 days. However, visa requirements and application processes can vary depending on your nationality, the purpose of your visit, and the length of your stay. You can check the requirements for your specific situation on the website of the Colombian Embassy or Consulate in your home country.

If you do require a visa, you will need to submit a completed visa application form, a passport photo, and any required supporting documents, such as a letter of invitation or a travel itinerary. Processing times for visas can vary, so it is recommended to apply well in advance of your travel date.

Electronic Travel Authorization:

Visitors from some countries may require an Electronic Travel Authorization (ETA) or a Reciprocity Fee to enter Colombia. The ETA is available online and can be obtained prior to your travel date. The Reciprocity Fee must be paid upon arrival in Colombia.

Yellow Fever Vaccination:

If you are traveling to Colombia from a country where yellow fever is present, you may be required to show proof of yellow fever vaccination. This is to prevent the spread of the disease to Colombia. It is recommended to check the vaccination requirements for your travel route and ensure you have the necessary vaccinations prior to departure.

In summary, when planning your visit to Colombia, ensure that your passport is valid for at least six months beyond your planned departure date, and check the visa and vaccination requirements for your specific situation. By being prepared and meeting the requirements, you can enjoy a smooth and stress-free travel experience in Colombia.

Travel insurance options

Travel insurance is an important consideration for any traveler, including those visiting Colombia. Here's what you need to know about travel insurance options for Colombia:

Why You Need Travel Insurance for Colombia: Travel insurance provides financial protection and peace of mind in case of unexpected events, such as medical emergencies, trip cancellations, or lost or stolen baggage. In Colombia, you may also want to consider travel insurance to cover potential risks such as natural disasters or civil unrest.

Types of Travel Insurance: There are several types of travel insurance available for visitors to Colombia, including:

1. Medical Travel Insurance: This type of insurance covers the cost of medical treatment, hospitalization, and emergency medical evacuation in case of illness or injury during your trip.

2. Trip Cancellation and Interruption Insurance: This type of insurance provides coverage for non-refundable trip expenses, such as flights and accommodations, in case of trip cancellation or interruption due to unforeseen events, such as illness, injury, or natural disasters.

3. Baggage and Personal Effects Insurance: This type of insurance provides coverage for lost, stolen, or damaged luggage and personal items during your trip.

4. Adventure Travel Insurance: This type of insurance is designed for travelers participating in adventure activities such as hiking, scuba diving, or skiing, and provides coverage for medical emergencies, equipment loss or damage, and trip cancellation or interruption related to adventure activities.

Where to Buy Travel Insurance: You can purchase travel insurance from a variety of sources, including:

1. Travel Insurance Companies: There are many companies that specialize in travel insurance, such as World Nomads, Allianz Global Assistance, and Travel Guard.

2. Travel Agencies: Many travel agencies offer travel insurance as an add-on to their travel packages.

3. Credit Card Companies: Some credit card companies offer travel insurance as a benefit to their cardholders.

4. Insurance Brokers: Insurance brokers can help you compare travel insurance options from different companies to find the best coverage for your needs.

When buying travel insurance, it is important to carefully read the policy terms and conditions to ensure that the coverage meets your specific needs. You should also be aware of any exclusions or limitations in the policy, such as pre-existing medical conditions or adventure activity exclusions.

In summary, travel insurance is an important consideration for anyone planning to visit Colombia. By understanding the types of coverage available and where to purchase it, you can ensure that you are protected in case of unexpected events during your trip.

Booking flights and accommodations

When planning a trip to Colombia, one of the most important decisions you'll make is booking your flights and accommodations. Here are some tips to help you make the best choices for your trip:

Booking Flights:

1. Start Early: The earlier you start looking for flights, the better chance you have of finding good deals. Aim to start looking at least 3-6 months before your planned travel dates.

2. Use Flight Comparison Websites: Use websites such as Skyscanner, Expedia, or Kayak to compare prices and find the best deals.

3. Be Flexible with Your Travel Dates: Being flexible with your travel dates can save you money. Try to avoid traveling during peak seasons, holidays, and weekends.

4. Consider Different Airports: Consider flying into smaller airports or airports that are a little further away from your destination, as they may offer lower fares.

5. Check for Special Deals: Keep an eye out for special deals and promotions offered by airlines, such as last-minute sales, student discounts, or reward programs.

6. Book Directly with Airlines: Booking directly with airlines can sometimes be cheaper than booking through third-party websites. Plus, it may offer better customer service in case of flight cancellations or changes.

Booking Accommodations:

1. Research Your Options: Do your research on the different types of accommodations available, such as hotels, hostels, guesthouses, or vacation rentals. Consider the location, amenities, and price when making your choice.

2. Read Reviews: Read reviews from other travelers to get a sense of the quality and service of the accommodations you're considering. Websites such as Trip advisor or Booking.com are great resources for reviews.

3. Use Booking Websites: Use booking websites such as Booking.com, Agoda, or Airbnb to compare prices and find the best deals.

4. Book in Advance: Book your accommodations in advance to avoid the risk of them being fully booked during peak travel seasons.

5. Consider Alternative Options: Consider alternative options such as house-sitting, Couchsurfing, or camping, if you're looking for a more budget-friendly or unique travel experience.

6. Be Aware of Cancellation Policies: Be aware of cancellation policies and any fees that may apply if you need to cancel or change your reservations.

7. Communicate with Your Host: If you're booking a vacation rental or staying with a host, communicate with them before your trip to ensure that everything is set up for your arrival.

Overall, booking flights and accommodations for your trip to Colombia requires careful planning and research. By following these tips, you can find the best deals and accommodations to fit your budget and travel preferences

Planning transportation and Itineraries

When planning your trip to Colombia, transportation and itinerary planning are two key factors to consider. Here are some tips to help you plan transportation and create a great itinerary for your trip:

Planning Transportation:

1. Research Your Options: Research the different transportation options available in Colombia, such as buses, taxis, trains, and planes. Consider the distance you need to travel and the time it will take to get there when choosing the best mode of transportation.

2. Book in Advance: Book transportation in advance to ensure that you have a seat and avoid the risk of tickets being sold out during peak travel seasons.

3. Consider Safety: Consider safety when choosing transportation options. Stick to reputable companies, avoid traveling alone at night, and be aware of your surroundings at all times.

4. Be Prepared for the Unexpected: Be prepared for unexpected delays or cancellations by having a backup plan in place. Keep important documents, such as your passport and travel insurance information, with you at all times.

5. Consider a Rental Car: Consider renting a car to give you the flexibility to explore at your own pace. However, be aware of the driving conditions in Colombia and any necessary permits or licenses needed to drive.

Creating an Itinerary:

1. Research Destinations: Research the different destinations in Colombia and create a list of the places you want to visit. Consider the time and distance it will take to travel between destinations and the activities you want to do in each place.

2. Prioritize Your Activities: Prioritize your activities based on your interests and the amount of time you have in each destination. Consider adding some downtime to your itinerary to relax and recharge.

3. Be Realistic: Be realistic about the amount of time you have and how much you can realistically fit into your itinerary. Don't try to cram too much into one day, as it can be exhausting and take away from the enjoyment of your trip.

4. Leave Room for Flexibility: Leave room for flexibility in your itinerary to allow for unexpected delays or to add activities you discover along the way.

5. Consider a Guided Tour: Consider joining a guided tour to help you navigate and make the most of your time in each destination. This can also provide you with valuable information about the culture and history of each place.

6. Include Local Experiences: Include local experiences in your itinerary to get a taste of the culture and way of life in Colombia. This could include trying local cuisine, attending cultural festivals, or participating in outdoor activities such as hiking or surfing.

Sample Itinerary for a 10-Day Trip to Colombia:

- Day 1-2: Bogotá - Visit the historic La Candelaria district, the Gold Museum, and take a cable car to the top of Monserrate for panoramic views of the city.
- Day 3-4: Medellín - Explore the vibrant city center, visit the Botanical Gardens, and take a day trip to the nearby town of Guatapé to see the colorful zocalos.
- Day 5-6: Cartagena - Explore the colonial Old Town, walk along the city walls, and visit the San Felipe Castle.
- Day 7-8: Santa Marta/Tayrona National Park - Relax on the beaches of Santa Marta and take a day trip to the stunning Tayrona National Park to hike and swim in the Caribbean Sea.
- Day 9-10: Coffee Region - Explore the picturesque towns of Salento and Filandia, visit a coffee plantation, and hike in the Cocora Valley to see the towering wax palms.

Overall, transportation and itinerary planning are essential for a successful trip to Colombia. By researching your options and creating a well-planned itinerary, you can make the most of your time in this beautiful country.

Budgeting for the trip

Budgeting for a trip to Colombia is an important aspect of travel preparations. Here are some tips to help you plan and manage your budget for your trip:

1. Determine Your Travel Dates: Determine when you plan to travel to Colombia, as prices for flights, accommodations, and activities can vary depending on the time of year.

2. Research Flight Prices: Research flight prices to Colombia from your location and determine the most cost-effective time to travel. Consider booking in advance or taking advantage of last-minute deals.

3. Consider Accommodations: Consider your accommodation options, such as hostels, hotels, or vacation rentals. Hostels are often the most affordable option, but may lack some amenities. Hotels and vacation rentals offer more comfort and amenities but can be more expensive.

4. Plan Your Itinerary: Plan your itinerary and activities in advance to get a better idea of how much money you will need for your trip. Consider the cost of transportation, entrance fees, and meals.

5. Set a Daily Budget: Set a daily budget for your trip, including accommodation, transportation, food, and activities. This will help you stay on track and avoid overspending.

6. Exchange Currency: Research the exchange rate for your currency and exchange your money before your trip. Consider using ATMs in Colombia to withdraw cash, as they often offer the best exchange rates.

7. Use Credit Cards Wisely: Use credit cards wisely and only for larger purchases. Many places in Colombia only accept cash, and using credit cards can lead to foreign transaction fees and additional charges.

8. Eat Like a Local: Eating like a local can help you save money on food costs. Look for street food vendors and local restaurants for affordable meals.

9. Take Advantage of Free Activities: Take advantage of free activities such as hiking, walking tours, and exploring museums and cultural sites.

10. Factor in Additional Expenses: Factor in additional expenses such as travel insurance, visas, and vaccinations.

Sample Budget for a 10-Day Trip to Colombia:

- Flight: $600
- Accommodations: $300 (hostels or budget hotels)
- Transportation: $150 (local buses, taxis, and flights between cities)
- Food: $200 (eating at local restaurants and street food vendors)
- Activities: $250 (entrance fees, tours, and other activities)
- Miscellaneous expenses: $100 (ATM fees, tips, and other small expenses)
- Total: $1,600

By following these tips and creating a budget for your trip to Colombia, you can have a memorable and affordable travel experience. Remember to stay flexible and adjust your budget as needed throughout your trip.

Health and Safety

Vaccinations and health precautions

When preparing to travel to Colombia, it is important to take into consideration the necessary vaccinations and health precautions to ensure a safe and healthy trip. Here are some important points to keep in mind:

- Consult with Your Doctor: Before traveling to Colombia, it is recommended that you consult with your doctor to discuss any potential health risks and recommended vaccinations.
- Vaccinations: It is recommended that travelers to Colombia be up-to-date on routine vaccinations such as measles, mumps, rubella, and polio. Other recommended vaccinations may include hepatitis A and B, typhoid, yellow fever, and rabies. The specific vaccinations you may need will depend on factors such as your age, health, and itinerary.
- Yellow Fever Vaccination: The yellow fever vaccine is required for travelers entering Colombia from countries where yellow fever is endemic. It is recommended to get the vaccine at least 10 days before traveling.
- Malaria: Malaria is present in some areas of Colombia, particularly in rural areas below 1,700 meters in altitude. It is recommended to take preventive measures such as antimalarial medication and insect repellent.
- Zika Virus: The Zika virus has been reported in Colombia, particularly in pregnant women. It is recommended to take measures to prevent mosquito bites, such as using insect repellent and wearing long sleeves and pants.
- Food and Water Safety: It is important to take precautions with food and water to avoid illness. Avoid drinking tap water and only consume water that has been boiled or bottled. Avoid consuming street food, uncooked food, or food from unreliable sources.
- Altitude Sickness: Altitude sickness can occur in high altitude areas such as Bogota, Medellin, and Cartagena. Symptoms may include headache, nausea, dizziness, and shortness of breath. It is

recommended to acclimate slowly to high altitudes and drink plenty of water.

- Travel Health Insurance: Consider purchasing travel health insurance to cover any medical expenses or emergency medical evacuation.

In summary, it is important to take necessary vaccinations and health precautions before traveling to Colombia. Consult with your doctor, research your itinerary and potential health risks, and take preventive measures to ensure a safe and healthy trip.

Medical insurance and emergency services

Medical insurance and emergency services are important aspects to consider when traveling to Colombia. Here are some important points to keep in mind:

- Medical Insurance: It is highly recommended to have medical insurance when traveling to Colombia. This will ensure that you are covered in case of any medical emergencies or accidents. Some travel insurance policies may include coverage for medical expenses and emergency medical evacuation.

- Emergency Services: In case of a medical emergency, you can call the emergency services number in Colombia which is 123. In major cities, private medical facilities are available, but in remote areas, the nearest hospital may be far away. It is important to have a plan in case of emergency and be aware of the location of the nearest hospital or medical facility.

- Prescription Medications: If you are traveling with prescription medications, it is recommended to bring a copy of your prescription and a letter from your doctor. This will help you to avoid any issues with customs officials and will also be helpful in case you need to refill your prescription while in Colombia.

- Language Barrier: In case of a medical emergency, it is important to be aware of the language barrier. Most doctors and medical staff in Colombia speak Spanish, so it is recommended to have a translator or to learn some basic Spanish phrases to communicate your needs.

- Emergency Medical Evacuation: If you require emergency medical evacuation, it is important to have the appropriate insurance coverage. Emergency medical evacuation can be expensive, so it is recommended to purchase travel insurance that includes this coverage.
- Medical Facilities: Medical facilities in Colombia can vary in quality, with the best hospitals and clinics being located in major cities. Private hospitals and clinics generally have better facilities and equipment than public hospitals. Before traveling to Colombia, research the medical facilities in the areas you plan to visit to be aware of the options available.

In summary, it is important to have medical insurance and be aware of emergency services when traveling to Colombia. It is recommended to have a plan in case of emergency and to research medical facilities in advance to be aware of the options available.

Travel advisories and warnings

When planning a trip to Colombia, it is important to be aware of travel advisories and warnings issued by your home country and the Colombian government. Here are some important points to keep in mind:

1. Crime: Colombia has a high crime rate, especially in some areas of the country. Travelers should be aware of their surroundings and avoid high crime areas. It is recommended to travel in groups, especially at night, and to avoid carrying large sums of cash or valuable items.

2. Terrorism: Although the number of terrorist attacks in Colombia has decreased in recent years, there is still a risk of terrorism. Travelers should be aware of their surroundings and avoid large gatherings or demonstrations. It is also recommended to be aware of the location of the nearest embassy or consulate.

3. Natural Disasters: Colombia is prone to natural disasters such as earthquakes, floods, and landslides. Travelers should be aware of the risks and follow any instructions or warnings issued by local authorities.

4. Political Unrest: Political demonstrations and strikes can occur in Colombia, and can sometimes turn violent. Travelers should avoid participating in demonstrations and be aware of the situation in the areas they plan to visit.

5. Health Risks: Colombia has a number of health risks, including Zika virus, dengue fever, and malaria. Travelers should take appropriate measures to prevent mosquito bites and should consult a healthcare provider before traveling to ensure they have the necessary vaccinations and medications.

6. Travel Advisories: Your home country may issue travel advisories or warnings for Colombia. It is important to review these advisories before traveling and to follow any recommendations or guidelines provided.

In summary, when traveling to Colombia it is important to be aware of the risks and to take appropriate measures to ensure your safety. Travelers should be aware of the crime rate, the risk of terrorism, natural disasters, political unrest, and health risks. It is recommended to follow any travel advisories or warnings issued by your home country or the Colombian government.

Safety Tips For Solo And Group Travel

Colombia is a beautiful country with a lot to offer travelers, but safety concerns can be a deterrent for some. Whether you are traveling solo or in a group, here are some safety tips to keep in mind when visiting Colombia:

1. Research your destination: Before traveling to Colombia, it is important to research the specific areas you plan to visit. Some areas of the country have higher crime rates and may be more dangerous than others. Make sure to read up on safety tips and travel advisories for the region you plan to visit.

2. Avoid flashy displays of wealth: In Colombia, it is important to be aware of your surroundings and avoid drawing attention to yourself. Avoid wearing expensive jewelry or carrying large sums of cash, and keep your valuables in a secure location.

3. Stay in well-lit areas: Whether you are traveling solo or in a group, it is important to stay in well-lit areas, especially at night. Avoid walking alone in unfamiliar areas, and consider using transportation services like taxis or ride-sharing apps.

4. Keep your documents safe: Make sure to keep your passport, identification, and other important documents in a safe and secure location. It is also recommended to make copies of these documents in case they are lost or stolen.

5. Stay connected: When traveling solo, it can be helpful to stay connected with friends and family back home. Make sure to have a working phone and to check in regularly with loved ones.

6. Use reputable transportation services: When using transportation services in Colombia, make sure to use reputable companies and avoid unmarked taxis or other unofficial services.

7. Learn some Spanish: Knowing some basic Spanish can be helpful when traveling in Colombia. It can make it easier to communicate with locals and can also help you avoid potential misunderstandings.

8. Avoid drugs and other illegal activities: Drug use and other illegal activities are not only dangerous, but they can also land you in legal trouble. Avoid participating in any activities that are illegal or that could put you at risk.

9. Trust your instincts: If something feels off or unsafe, trust your instincts and remove yourself from the situation. It is always better to err on the side of caution when it comes to your safety.

10. Use common sense: Finally, use common sense when traveling in Colombia. Be aware of your surroundings, stay in well-lit areas, and avoid potentially dangerous situations.

In summary, traveling to Colombia can be a safe and enjoyable experience if you take the necessary precautions. Whether you are traveling solo or in a group, make sure to research your destination, avoid flashy displays of wealth, stay in well-lit areas, keep your documents safe, stay connected with loved ones, use reputable transportation services, learn some Spanish, avoid drugs and other illegal activities, trust your instincts, and use common sense. By following these safety tips, you can enjoy all that Colombia has to offer while staying safe and secure.

Dealing with emergencies and unexpected situations

While we all hope for smooth travels, emergencies and unexpected situations can happen. Being prepared and knowing what to do can make a big difference in how you handle these situations. Here are some tips for dealing with emergencies and unexpected situations while traveling in Colombia:

1. Keep emergency contact information on hand: Before you leave on your trip, make sure to have important phone numbers and contact information for local emergency services, your embassy or consulate, and your travel insurance provider. Keep this information in a safe and easily accessible location.

2. Have a plan for communication: If you are traveling with others, make sure to have a plan for communication in case you become separated. This can include agreeing on a meeting point or setting up a group chat.

3. Know basic first aid: Knowing basic first aid can be helpful in emergency situations. Consider taking a first aid course before your trip or at least reviewing basic techniques such as CPR and wound care.

4. Have a backup plan for accommodations: In case of unexpected situations such as flight cancellations or overbooked hotels, it's always good to have a backup plan for accommodations. Consider booking a refundable or flexible reservation or having a list of alternative accommodations in your budget.

5. Be aware of your surroundings: Staying aware of your surroundings can help you avoid potential dangers and situations. Pay attention to your surroundings and trust your instincts. If a situation feels off, remove yourself from it.

6. Contact your embassy or consulate: If you find yourself in a serious emergency, such as losing your passport, getting arrested, or needing medical attention, contact your embassy or consulate. They can provide assistance and guidance on how to proceed.

7. Know your insurance coverage: Make sure to review your travel insurance coverage before your trip and understand what is and isn't covered. In case of emergency situations such as medical issues, accidents or thefts, contact your insurance company immediately for instructions.

8. Have cash on hand: In case of emergencies, it's always a good idea to have some cash on hand. This can help you pay for unexpected expenses or transportation in case of emergencies.

9. Stay calm: Finally, it's important to stay calm in emergency situations. Panic can make things worse, so take deep breaths and try to think clearly about the situation.

In summary, dealing with emergencies and unexpected situations while traveling in Colombia requires preparation and quick thinking. Make sure to have emergency contact information on hand, a plan for communication, basic first aid knowledge, a backup plan for accommodations, awareness of surroundings, and cash on hand. Additionally, contact your embassy or consulate in case of serious emergencies and know your insurance coverage. Most importantly, stay calm and take things one step at a time. With these tips, you can handle unexpected situations with confidence and peace of mind.

CHAPTER TWO
Cultural Awareness and Etiquette

Understanding the local culture and customs
Colombia is a country with a rich cultural heritage and diverse customs. Understanding and respecting the local culture can enhance your travel experience and help you connect with the people and places you visit. Here are some key aspects of Colombian culture and customs to keep in mind:

1. Language: Spanish is the official language of Colombia, and it is spoken by the vast majority of the population. While many Colombians speak some English, it's always a good idea to learn some basic Spanish phrases to communicate with locals and navigate daily life.

2. Religion: Colombia is a predominantly Catholic country, with over 70% of the population identifying as Catholic. Other religions such as Protestantism and Islam are also present, as well as indigenous beliefs and practices.

3. Greetings: Colombians are friendly and hospitable people, and greetings are an important part of their culture. Handshakes are the most common form of greeting, and it's polite to use formal titles such as "señor" or "señora" when addressing someone you don't know well. Friends and family often greet each other with hugs or cheek kisses.

4. Family: Family is at the center of Colombian culture, and strong family ties are highly valued. It's common for extended family members to live together and support each other.

5. Food: Colombian cuisine is diverse and flavorful, with regional specialties and influences from indigenous, African, and Spanish cultures. Popular dishes include arepas (corn cakes), empanadas (fried or baked turnovers), and bandeja paisa (a hearty platter with rice, beans, meat, and avocado).

6. Music and dance: Music and dance are integral parts of Colombian culture, with a wide variety of styles and rhythms. The most famous dance is the salsa, which originated in the Caribbean coast of

Colombia. Other popular styles include cumbia, vallenato, and champeta.

7. Festivals and celebrations: Colombia is known for its vibrant festivals and celebrations, which are often religious or cultural in nature. Some of the most famous include the Carnival of Barranquilla, the Flower Fair in Medellin, and the Feria de Cali.

8. Clothing: Traditional Colombian clothing varies by region and reflects the country's diverse cultural heritage. For example, in the Andean region, women often wear colorful skirts, shawls, and hats, while men wear ponchos and woolen hats.

9. Social norms: Colombians value politeness and respect, and it's important to be aware of social norms when interacting with locals. For example, it's considered rude to interrupt someone while they are speaking, and it's polite to wait for an invitation before entering someone's home.

10. Safety and security: While Colombia has made great strides in improving its safety and security in recent years, it's still important to take precautions to stay safe while traveling. This includes avoiding high-crime areas, staying aware of your surroundings, and keeping your valuables secure.

In summary, understanding the local culture and customs is an important aspect of travel in Colombia. Learning some basic Spanish phrases, respecting social norms, and being aware of local customs related to food, music, and celebrations can enhance your travel experience and help you connect with the people and places you visit. By taking the time to learn about Colombian culture, you'll gain a deeper appreciation for this fascinating country and its people.

Learning basic language phrases

Learning basic language phrases can greatly enhance your travel experience in Colombia by allowing you to better communicate with locals and gain a deeper understanding of their culture. While English is widely spoken in popular tourist destinations, especially in big cities, knowing some Spanish phrases can be helpful in smaller towns and more rural areas.

Here are 50 essential Spanish phrases to help you get by during your travels in Colombia:

1. Hola - Hello

2. Buenos días - Good morning

3. Buenas tardes - Good afternoon

4. Buenas noches - Good evening

5. ¿Cómo estás? - How are you?

6. Estoy bien, gracias. ¿Y tú? - I'm fine, thank you. And you?

7. Mucho gusto - Nice to meet you

8. ¿Cómo te llamas? - What's your name?

9. Me llamo... - My name is...

10. Por favor - Please

11. Gracias - Thank you

12. De nada - You're welcome

13. Lo siento - I'm sorry

14. ¿Hablas inglés? - Do you speak English?

15. No hablo español muy bien - I don't speak Spanish very well

16. ¿Dónde está el baño? - Where is the bathroom?

17. ¿Cuánto cuesta? - How much does it cost?

18. ¿Puede ayudarme? - Can you help me?

19. Necesito ayuda - I need help

20. No entiendo - I don't understand

21. ¿Qué hora es? - What time is it?

22. ¿Dónde está...? - Where is...?

23. La cuenta, por favor - The bill, please

24. ¿Qué recomiendas? - What do you recommend?

25. Quiero ordenar - I'd like to order

26. ¿Tienes...? - Do you have...?

27. Sin hielo - Without ice

28. Con hielo - With ice

29. Agua sin gas - Still water

30. Agua con gas - Sparkling water

31. Vino tinto - Red wine

32. Vino blanco - White wine

33. Cerveza - Beer

34. ¿Aceptas tarjetas de crédito? - Do you accept credit cards?

35. No aceptamos tarjetas de crédito - We don't accept credit cards

36. ¿Puedo pagar en efectivo? - Can I pay in cash?

37. El menú, por favor - The menu, please

38. ¿Está incluido el servicio? - Is the service included?

39. No incluye el servicio - The service is not included

40. La propina - The tip

41. El aeropuerto - The airport

42. La estación de autobuses - The bus station

43. La estación de trenes - The train station

44. La calle - The street

45. La plaza - The square

46. El museo - The museum

47. La playa - The beach

48. La montaña - The mountain

49. El río - The river

50. El parque - The park

Remember, these are just some basic phrases to help you get by during your travels in Colombia. Learning more Spanish can only enhance your experience and allow you to connect with locals on a deeper level. Additionally, it is always a good idea to bring a Spanish phrasebook or download a translation app on your phone for easy reference.

Dress code and appropriate behavior

When traveling to Colombia, it is important to take into account the climate and dress appropriately. The country has a tropical climate, but its geography and altitude cause significant variations in temperature and rainfall. Understanding the weather patterns and dress codes for different regions will ensure you are comfortable and properly dressed for your trip.

In general, Colombians tend to dress well and are mindful of their appearance. While there is no strict dress code, it is important to dress appropriately for different situations and occasions. Here are some tips on dressing appropriately for different weather conditions and social situations:

1. Hot and humid weather: Colombia has a tropical climate, with temperatures ranging from 24 to 28°C (75 to 82°F) on average. The coastal areas can be hotter and more humid, with temperatures ranging from 28 to 32°C (82 to 90°F). Lightweight and breathable fabrics such as cotton, linen, and rayon are recommended. Shorts, sundresses, and skirts are acceptable in most settings, but it is important to dress modestly in certain places such as churches or government buildings. Sunscreen, a hat, and sunglasses are also recommended to protect against the sun's rays.

2. Rainy season: Colombia has two rainy seasons - from April to June and from October to November. During these months, it is important to have a rain jacket or umbrella on hand. Waterproof footwear is also recommended. In the cities, you can wear lightweight rain jackets or ponchos, while in the countryside, it is best to have a more robust jacket or poncho.

3. Cold weather: Some regions of Colombia, such as Bogota and the Andes Mountains, have cooler temperatures. Average temperatures range from 12 to 18°C (54 to 64°F) in these areas, but it can get much

colder at higher elevations. It is important to dress in layers, including a warm jacket, sweater, and scarf. Hats and gloves may also be necessary. In the evenings, temperatures can drop significantly, so it is best to be prepared.

4. Social occasions: Colombians tend to dress well for social occasions. Formal events such as weddings or business meetings may require suits or cocktail dresses. Casual events such as dinners or parties may allow for more relaxed attire, such as jeans and a nice shirt. When in doubt, it is always best to err on the side of dressing up rather than dressing down.

When it comes to behavior, Colombians are generally friendly and hospitable. They place a high value on personal relationships and are very family-oriented. Here are some tips to ensure you behave appropriately while traveling in Colombia:

1. Greetings: Colombians greet each other with a kiss on the cheek and a handshake. It is important to maintain eye contact while greeting someone and to address them by their title or last name until they invite you to use their first name.

2. Punctuality: Colombians are generally punctual, but social events may start later than the scheduled time. It is important to be respectful of other people's time and to arrive on time.

3. Personal space: Colombians tend to stand close to each other while speaking. It is important to respect personal space and not to invade someone's personal bubble.

4. Respect for elders: Colombians place a high value on respect for elders. It is important to address older people with respect and deference.

5. Language: While Spanish is the official language of Colombia, there are many regional dialects and variations. Learning basic phrases in Spanish can go a long way in establishing a connection with locals and making your trip more enjoyable.

Additionally, it's important to note that Colombia is a country with a diverse climate, which can vary depending on the region and the time of year. In general, the country has a tropical climate, with high temperatures and humidity levels. However, there are significant differences in temperature and rainfall depending on the region.

When traveling to Colombia, it's essential to pack appropriate clothing and gear for the climate and activities you plan to undertake. In coastal areas, such as Cartagena and Santa Marta, temperatures can reach over 30 degrees Celsius (86°F) year-round. Here, light, breathable clothing and sunscreen are a must. In the Andean regions, such as Bogotá and Medellín, temperatures are cooler and can drop to around 10 degrees Celsius (50°F) at night. Therefore, it's important to pack layers and warm clothing.

During the rainy season (April to June and September to November), it's important to pack waterproof clothing, umbrellas, and rain boots. In contrast, the dry season (December to March and July to August) tends to be hotter and drier. It's essential to stay hydrated and pack sunscreen, hats, and sunglasses to protect against the sun.

When it comes to appropriate behavior for Colombian travelers, it's important to remember that Colombia is a country with a rich culture and traditions. Colombians are generally friendly and welcoming, and visitors are usually greeted with warmth and hospitality. However, it's essential to show respect for the local culture and customs.

For example, it's important to dress appropriately when visiting religious sites and other cultural landmarks. Wearing shorts and tank tops may not be appropriate, and it's better to err on the side of conservatism. Additionally, it's important to be respectful of personal space and cultural norms. Avoid touching people or objects without permission, and be mindful of local customs and traditions.

In conclusion, understanding the local culture and customs is an essential part of travel preparation to Colombia. By learning about the local customs and traditions, travelers can better enjoy their trip and avoid misunderstandings. Additionally, packing appropriate clothing and gear for the climate and activities planned can make a significant difference in the comfort and enjoyment of the trip.

Food and drink etiquette

Colombia is a country with a rich culinary tradition, influenced by its diverse geography and cultural heritage. From hearty stews to fresh ceviche, there is no shortage of delicious food and drink to enjoy during your trip to Colombia. In this section, we'll explore some of the most popular dishes and drinks in Colombia, as well as food and drink etiquette.

What to Eat in Colombia

1. Bandeja Paisa: This hearty dish is a staple of Colombian cuisine and is popular in the Andean region. The dish includes rice, beans, ground beef, chicharron (pork rinds), fried egg, avocado, plantain, and arepa (a type of corn cake).

2. Empanadas: Empanadas are a popular snack in Colombia, made from a corn or wheat flour dough filled with meat, cheese, or vegetables. They are typically fried until golden brown and served with aji, a spicy salsa.

3. Arepas: Arepas are a type of corn cake that is popular in Colombia and other Latin American countries. They are made from cornmeal and can be stuffed with meat, cheese, or vegetables.

4. Sancocho: This hearty soup is a staple of Colombian cuisine and is often served during special occasions. The soup includes chicken, plantain, yucca, corn, and other vegetables.

5. Ceviche: Ceviche is a popular seafood dish in Colombia, made from raw fish marinated in lime juice and served with onions, tomatoes, and cilantro.

What to Drink in Colombia

1. Coffee: Colombia is known for its high-quality coffee, and a trip to Colombia is not complete without trying a cup of locally grown coffee.

2. Aguardiente: Aguardiente is a popular anise-flavored liquor in Colombia, often consumed during celebrations and social events.

3. Chicha: Chicha is a traditional fermented drink made from maize or yucca that is popular in the Andean region.

4. Fruit Juices: Colombia is home to a wide variety of tropical fruits, and fresh fruit juices are a popular and refreshing drink.

Food and Drink Etiquette in Colombia

Colombians are generally hospitable and enjoy sharing their culinary traditions with visitors. However, there are a few food and drink etiquette rules to keep in mind when traveling to Colombia.

1. Respect the host: If you are invited to a Colombian's home for a meal, it is important to arrive on time and bring a small gift such as flowers or chocolates. It is also polite to compliment the host on the food and drink.

2. Use utensils: In Colombia, it is customary to eat with utensils rather than with your hands, except when eating empanadas or arepas. It is also considered rude to speak with food in your mouth.

3. Finish what's on your plate: In Colombia, it is considered impolite to leave food on your plate. It's better to take smaller portions and ask for seconds than to leave food uneaten.

4. Toasts: Toasting is an important part of socializing in Colombia. When toasting, it is customary to make eye contact with the person you are toasting and clink glasses. It's also polite to toast the host or the occasion.

5. Offer to pay: When dining out with friends or colleagues, it is polite to offer to pay for your share of the meal. It is also customary for the host to pay for the meal, especially if they have invited you.

In conclusion, food and drink are an essential part of Colombian culture, and travelers should take advantage of the opportunity to try traditional dishes and beverages. By respecting local customs and etiquette, travelers can enjoy their meals and drinks while making a positive impression

Respect for religious and political beliefs

Colombia is a diverse country with a rich cultural heritage. As such, it is essential to be mindful of the various religious and political beliefs that exist in the country. While Colombia is primarily a Roman Catholic country, it is also home to several other religions such as Protestantism, Evangelicalism, Judaism, and Islam, among others.

It is essential to show respect for these religions and their beliefs, especially when visiting their worship centers. Visitors should dress modestly, remove their shoes before entering the worship center, and observe any other specific requirements that may exist. Visitors should also be aware that some religious sites may be closed to non-believers during certain times, and it is crucial to observe these restrictions.

The primary religion in Colombia is Roman Catholicism, and there are several beautiful churches and cathedrals throughout the country. One of the most famous is the Cathedral of Our Lady of the Rosary in Popayán, which is a UNESCO World Heritage Site. Another significant Catholic site is the Basilica of the Lord of Miracles in Buga, which is the second most important pilgrimage site in Latin America, after the Basilica of Our Lady of Guadalupe in Mexico City.

Protestantism and Evangelicalism have gained significant popularity in Colombia in recent years, with many churches spread throughout the country. Some of the most notable ones include the Iglesia Cristiana de Restauración in Bogotá and the Iglesia de Dios Pentecostal in Cali.

Islam is a minority religion in Colombia, with a small but growing Muslim community. The country has several mosques, with the most prominent being the Centro Islámico de Colombia in Bogotá.

Judaism is also a minority religion in Colombia, with a small but active community. The largest synagogue in the country is the Sinagoga Shaare Shalom in Barranquilla.

Colombia has a diverse and dynamic political scene, with several political parties and ideologies. It is essential to be respectful of these beliefs, especially when discussing politics with locals. Visitors should avoid engaging in heated political discussions, especially if they are not familiar with the local political climate.

In conclusion, visitors to Colombia should be respectful of the diverse religious and political beliefs that exist in the country. They should take the time to learn about these beliefs and the cultural customs associated with them. By doing so, they can better understand the country and its people and enjoy a more meaningful and fulfilling travel experience.

Packing and Gear

Essential travel items and gadgets

When preparing for a trip to Colombia, it is important to ensure that you have all the necessary items and gadgets that you will need during your stay. Here are some essential travel items and gadgets to consider packing for your trip:

1. Travel documents: This includes your passport, visa, travel insurance documents, and any other important documents required for your trip.

2. Money and credit cards: Make sure to have some cash in the local currency, as well as credit and debit cards. It is also a good idea to have a money belt or pouch to keep your valuables safe.

3. Backpack or daypack: A sturdy backpack or daypack is essential for carrying your daily essentials such as water bottles, snacks, and camera.

4. Comfortable walking shoes: Colombia has a lot of beautiful places to explore, and comfortable walking shoes will ensure that you can walk around comfortably for long hours.

5. Lightweight clothing: The climate in Colombia is generally warm and humid, so pack lightweight clothing that is breathable and comfortable.

6. Sunscreen and insect repellent: Protect your skin from the harsh sun and insect bites by packing sunscreen and insect repellent.

7. Universal power adapter: If you plan to use electrical devices during your trip, bring a universal power adapter that can be used in Colombia.

8. Smartphone and charger: Your smartphone will come in handy for taking photos, navigating, and staying in touch with loved ones. Don't forget to pack a charger as well.

9. Portable battery pack: A portable battery pack will ensure that you never run out of charge for your electronic devices.

10. Spanish-English dictionary or translation app: Even if you are not fluent in Spanish, having a dictionary or translation app will help you communicate better with the locals.

11. Travel pillow and earplugs: Long flights and bus rides can be tiring, so pack a travel pillow and earplugs to help you sleep better.

12. Water bottle: Staying hydrated is important in Colombia's warm climate. Bring a reusable water bottle to fill up and reduce plastic waste.

13. First aid kit: Accidents can happen, so bring a basic first aid kit with essentials such as band-aids, antiseptic wipes, and pain relievers.

14. Camera: Colombia is a beautiful country with many picturesque locations. Bring a camera to capture your memories.

By packing these essential travel items and gadgets, you will be well prepared for your trip to Colombia and be able to fully enjoy all that this beautiful country has to offer.

Packing strategies and tips

Packing for a trip can be both exciting and overwhelming. However, with a good strategy and tips, you can make the process smooth and stress-free. Here are some packing strategies and tips to help you prepare for your trip to Colombia:

1. Make a packing list: Before you start packing, make a list of all the items you need to carry. This will help you stay organized and ensure you don't forget any important items.

2. Consider the weather: Colombia has a tropical climate, so it's usually warm and humid throughout the year. However, some regions can get

chilly, especially at night. Make sure you pack clothes that are suitable for the weather conditions in the regions you plan to visit.

3. Pack versatile clothing: It's important to pack clothes that can be worn in multiple ways. This will help you save space and also give you more options to mix and match your outfits.

4. Choose the right luggage: The type of luggage you choose can make a big difference in your packing experience. Consider factors such as durability, size, and weight when selecting your luggage.

5. Use packing cubes: Packing cubes are a great way to stay organized and keep your belongings in order. They also make it easier to find what you need without having to unpack everything.

6. Pack smart gadgets: Some useful gadgets to pack for your trip to Colombia include a power bank, universal adapter, portable charger, and a waterproof phone case.

7. Pack toiletries and medications: Don't forget to pack essential toiletries such as toothbrush, toothpaste, deodorant, and sunscreen. If you have any medications, make sure you carry them in their original packaging and bring a copy of your prescription.

8. Leave some space for souvenirs: If you plan to do some shopping while in Colombia, make sure you leave some space in your luggage for souvenirs and other items you may want to bring back home.

9. Wear your bulky items on the plane: If you have bulky items such as a jacket or boots, wear them on the plane to save space in your luggage.

10. Double-check before you leave: Before you leave for your trip, double-check your packing list to ensure you haven't forgotten anything. It's also a good idea to weigh your luggage to make sure it meets the airline's weight restrictions.

By following these packing strategies and tips, you can ensure a stress-free and organized packing experience for your trip to Colombia.

Choosing appropriate clothing and footwear

When it comes to packing for a trip to Colombia, it's important to consider the climate, local customs, and the activities you'll be participating in. Here are some tips for choosing appropriate clothing and footwear:

1. Check the weather: Colombia has a tropical climate, so be sure to pack light, breathable clothing for the hot and humid conditions. However, if you plan on traveling to higher elevations, such as Bogotá, you'll need to pack warmer clothing for the cooler temperatures.

2. Consider cultural norms: Colombia is a conservative country, so it's important to dress modestly, especially in religious sites and rural areas. Avoid wearing revealing clothing, such as shorts or tank tops, and opt for lightweight, long-sleeved tops and pants.

3. Choose comfortable footwear: Colombia's terrain can be rough, so be sure to pack comfortable, durable footwear that can handle walking on uneven surfaces. Sneakers, hiking shoes, and sandals with a good grip are good choices.

4. Pack layers: Colombia's climate can vary greatly from day to night and from region to region, so be sure to pack layers that can be easily added or removed as needed.

5. Consider your itinerary: If you plan on participating in outdoor activities such as hiking or zip-lining, be sure to pack appropriate clothing and footwear for these activities. You may also want to bring a rain jacket or poncho in case of inclement weather.

Overall, it's important to be mindful of local customs and climate when choosing what to pack for your trip to Colombia. With a little planning, you can ensure that you have the appropriate clothing and footwear for a comfortable and enjoyable trip

Carrying and securing valuables

Carrying and securing valuables is an essential aspect of travel preparations, especially in countries where pickpocketing and theft are prevalent. In Colombia, as with many other countries, it is important to take precautions to ensure the safety of your valuable items.

The first step in securing your valuables is to decide which items you need to bring with you and which ones you can leave behind. It is advisable to bring only the essential items that you need for your trip, leaving behind any items that are not necessary. This will not only make it easier to keep track of your belongings, but also reduce the risk of loss or theft.

When it comes to securing your valuables, there are a few strategies that you can use. Firstly, you should keep your valuables on your person at all times. This means keeping your wallet, phone, and other important items in a secure place such as a cross-body bag or a backpack that you can carry in front of you.

Another strategy is to use a money belt, which is a discreet way to carry your valuables. A money belt is a small pouch that is worn around the waist, underneath your clothing. It is ideal for carrying cash, credit cards, and important documents such as your passport. This way, even if your bag is stolen, your valuables will remain safe.

If you need to carry larger valuables such as cameras, laptops or tablets, it is recommended that you keep them in a secure bag that can be locked with a combination or key lock. This will make it more difficult for anyone to steal your valuable items.

It is important to note that some accommodation options may offer a safe for you to store your valuable items. If you are staying in a hotel, for example, you can ask the front desk if they have a safe that you can use.

In addition to these strategies, it is also important to be aware of your surroundings and take precautions when in crowded or busy areas. For example, avoid keeping your phone or wallet in your back pocket, as it is easier for pickpockets to access them in these areas. Always keep an eye on your belongings and be mindful of anyone who is standing too close or behaving suspiciously.

In conclusion, carrying and securing your valuables is an essential aspect of travel preparations. By using a combination of strategies such as keeping your valuables on your person, using a money belt, and locking your bags, you can help ensure that your valuable items remain safe and secure during your trip to Colombia.

Renting or buying gear at the destination

Renting or buying gear at the destination can be a great option for travelers who are looking to save space and money when packing for their trip to Colombia. This is especially true for those who plan to engage in activities such as hiking, camping, or water sports, which may require specialized equipment that is not practical to bring from home.

Here are some things to consider when deciding whether to rent or buy gear at your destination in Colombia:

1. Cost: The cost of renting or buying gear can vary depending on the type of equipment and the location. In general, renting gear is cheaper than buying, but it may not be the best option if you plan to use the equipment frequently or for an extended period of time. In contrast, buying gear may be more expensive upfront, but it can be more cost-effective in the long run.

2. Quality: When renting or buying gear, it's important to consider the quality of the equipment. In some cases, rental gear may be older or less well-maintained than gear you would purchase, which could impact your safety and comfort during your trip. On the other hand, buying lower-quality gear may result in needing to replace it sooner, which can be more costly in the long run.

3. Availability: Depending on where you are traveling in Colombia, it may be easier or more difficult to find rental equipment. For example, major cities like Bogotá or Medellin may have more options for renting gear, while smaller towns or rural areas may not have any rental services available. Similarly, if you have specific equipment needs, such as a particular size of wetsuit, it may be more difficult to find the right gear for rent.

4. Convenience: Renting gear can be a convenient option for travelers who don't want to worry about packing or transporting bulky equipment. However, if you plan to rent gear, you'll need to factor in the time and effort required to pick up and return the equipment, as well as any additional fees or deposits that may be required.

5. Sustainability: If you're concerned about the environmental impact of your travel, consider whether renting or buying gear is more sustainable. Renting gear can reduce waste and minimize the

resources required to produce and transport equipment, but it may also contribute to a culture of disposable consumerism. In contrast, buying high-quality gear that you can use for multiple trips can be a more sustainable option in the long run.

Overall, the decision to rent or buy gear at your destination in Colombia will depend on your specific needs and preferences. If you're planning a short trip or don't want to invest in expensive equipment, renting may be the best option. However, if you plan to use the equipment frequently or for an extended period of time, it may be more cost-effective to buy gear that you can use on multiple trips. Regardless of your choice, be sure to do your research and choose equipment that is safe, comfortable, and appropriate for your needs.

Money and Finances

Currency exchange and conversion rates
When travelling abroad, it's essential to understand the local currency and how to exchange it for your own currency. Colombia's official currency is the Colombian peso (COP), which is divided into 100 centavos. As with many countries, currency exchange rates in Colombia are subject to fluctuations in the global market, so it's crucial to keep an eye on the current rates before your trip.

Here are some tips to help you navigate currency exchange in Colombia:

1. Know the current exchange rate: Before you go to Colombia, research the current exchange rate so that you can determine how much money you need to bring and how much you can expect to get in exchange for your currency.

2. Choose a reputable exchange service: In Colombia, you can exchange money at banks, exchange houses, and some hotels. Look for reputable exchange services that offer fair rates and low commissions. Avoid exchanging money on the street or from unlicensed vendors, as this can be risky.

3. Be aware of fees: Some exchange services charge fees for their services. Be sure to ask about fees and commissions before making an exchange.

4. Use a credit card: Most major credit cards are widely accepted in Colombia, especially in larger cities and tourist areas. Using a credit card can be a convenient way to pay for purchases and avoid carrying large amounts of cash.

5. Withdraw money from ATMs: ATMs are widely available in Colombia, and they offer a convenient way to withdraw cash using your debit or credit card. Be sure to check with your bank about foreign transaction fees and withdrawal limits.

6. Be prepared to haggle: In Colombia, haggling is a common practice, especially in markets and with street vendors. Don't be afraid to negotiate the price of goods and services to get a fair deal.

7. Keep your money safe: When exchanging money or carrying cash, it's essential to keep your money safe. Consider using a money belt or a secure travel wallet to protect your valuables.

In summary, it's crucial to be prepared when it comes to currency exchange in Colombia. Do your research, choose reputable exchange services, and be aware of fees and commissions. By following these tips, you can ensure that you have a safe and enjoyable trip to Colombia.

Managing money and credit cards

When traveling to Colombia, it is important to have a plan for managing your money and credit cards. Here are some tips to help you stay on top of your finances while traveling:

1. Research currency exchange rates: Before leaving for your trip, research the current exchange rates between your home currency and the Colombian peso. This will help you better understand how much money you'll need for your trip and whether it's better to exchange currency at home or in Colombia.

2. Bring multiple forms of payment: It's always a good idea to bring multiple forms of payment, such as cash, credit cards, and debit cards. This way, you'll have backup options if one form of payment doesn't work or if you lose your wallet.

3. Notify your bank and credit card companies: Before leaving for your trip, make sure to notify your bank and credit card companies that you'll be traveling to Colombia. This will help prevent your accounts from being flagged for fraud and potentially frozen.

4. Use ATMs wisely: When withdrawing money from an ATM in Colombia, try to use one located inside a bank rather than on the street. This is because there is a higher risk of ATM skimming scams on street-side machines.

5. Keep cash and cards secure: Keep your cash and cards in separate places, such as a money belt and a separate wallet. This way, if one is stolen or lost, you still have access to your money.

6. Be aware of credit card fees: Some credit cards charge foreign transaction fees or ATM withdrawal fees. Check with your credit card company before your trip to see if there are any fees you should be aware of.

7. Consider using a travel credit card: If you frequently travel, consider getting a travel credit card. These cards often have perks such as no foreign transaction fees, travel rewards, and travel insurance.

Overall, managing your money and credit cards while traveling in Colombia requires some planning and attention to detail. By following these tips, you can help ensure that your finances stay in order while you enjoy all that Colombia has to offer.

Avoiding common scams and frauds

Travelling to a new country can be an exciting experience, but it is important to stay vigilant and aware of potential scams and frauds. Unfortunately, scammers and fraudsters exist everywhere, and Colombia is no exception. Being aware of common scams and frauds can help you avoid falling victim to them and ruining your trip.

Here are some common scams and frauds to watch out for in Colombia:

1. Fake Police Scams: Scammers posing as police officers may approach you on the street and ask to see your passport or ID. They may then claim that your documents are fake and demand a bribe. Always ask to see the officer's identification before handing over any documents, and if you suspect the person is not a real police officer, walk away and find a real officer or police station.

2. Street Scams: These types of scams involve distracting you while an accomplice steals your belongings. Common examples include someone spilling food or drink on you and then offering to help clean it up while their partner steals your wallet, or someone asking for directions and then taking advantage of your distraction to grab your bag or wallet. Be aware of your surroundings and keep your belongings close to you.

3. Money Exchange Scams: When exchanging money, always use authorized exchange offices or banks. Scammers may approach you

on the street and offer to exchange your money for a higher rate, but they will often use counterfeit bills or trick you into handing over more money than you should.

4. Tourist Scams: Some people may offer to take you on a tour or to a popular attraction, but then overcharge you or take you to a different, less desirable location. Always research reputable tour companies and attractions beforehand, and never hand over money until you have agreed on a price.

5. Credit Card Skimming: When paying with your credit card, be aware of where your card is being swiped. Scammers may use a skimming device to steal your credit card information, which can lead to unauthorized purchases on your account. Use cash when possible, or only use your card at reputable businesses.

To avoid falling victim to these scams and frauds, always be aware of your surroundings, keep your belongings close to you, and use common sense. If something seems too good to be true, it probably is. Stay safe and enjoy your trip to Colombia!

Tipping and bargaining practices

Tipping and bargaining practices can vary greatly from one country to another. When traveling to Colombia, it's important to be aware of the local customs and expectations when it comes to tipping and bargaining.

Tipping is not mandatory in Colombia, but it's becoming more common in tourist areas. In restaurants, a 10% service charge is usually added to the bill, but it's still customary to leave an additional 5-10% tip for good service. In bars, it's common to tip the bartender a small amount for each drink.

When it comes to other services, such as haircuts, massages, or tours, tipping is also appreciated but not mandatory. It's up to your discretion to decide on the amount to tip, but 5-10% of the total price is usually sufficient.

Bargaining is a common practice in Colombia, particularly in markets and street vendors. It's important to approach bargaining with respect and understanding of the local customs. It's not uncommon for vendors to quote a high price initially, expecting the buyer to negotiate down.

However, it's important to avoid being too aggressive in bargaining, as it can be seen as disrespectful.

When bargaining, it's important to start with a reasonable counteroffer and be willing to meet in the middle. It's also helpful to do some research beforehand to get an idea of what a fair price should be.

Overall, tipping and bargaining in Colombia require a delicate balance of respecting local customs and being aware of the value of the goods or services. With a little research and understanding, travelers can navigate these practices with ease.

Tax refunds and duty-free shopping

Tax refunds and duty-free shopping are important aspects of travel for many tourists. Knowing how to take advantage of tax refunds and duty-free shopping can save you a significant amount of money during your trip to Colombia.

Tax Refunds: Colombia has a Value Added Tax (VAT) of 19%, which is included in the price of most goods and services. Foreign tourists who make purchases in Colombia can be eligible for a tax refund on their purchases. To be eligible for a tax refund, the total value of the purchases made in Colombia must be greater than 1,050,000 COP (approximately $290 USD).

To obtain a tax refund, you must request a tax-free form (formulario tax-free) from the vendor at the time of purchase. This form must be completed and submitted to the DIAN (Colombia's tax authority) when you leave the country. The DIAN will verify the form and issue a refund within 30 days. The refund can be issued in cash, credited to a credit card, or deposited into a bank account.

Duty-Free Shopping: Duty-free shopping is available at most airports and seaports in Colombia. These shops offer a variety of products including liquor, tobacco, electronics, and luxury goods. Prices at duty-free shops are usually lower than retail prices in Colombia because they are exempt from local taxes and duties.

To purchase items at a duty-free shop, you must present a boarding pass for a flight leaving Colombia or a ticket for a cruise leaving the port. Some duty-free shops may also require a passport or other identification. Payment can be made with cash or credit card.

It is important to note that duty-free allowances vary by country, so it is important to check the allowances for your home country before making any purchases. Some items may also be restricted or prohibited, so it is important to check the regulations before making any purchases.

In conclusion, tax refunds and duty-free shopping can be great ways to save money during your trip to Colombia. It is important to familiarize yourself with the regulations and requirements for tax refunds and duty-free shopping to ensure that you are eligible and that you follow the necessary procedures.

CHAPTER THREE

Communication and Connectivity

Phone and internet options

When traveling to Colombia, it's important to stay connected with your loved ones, especially if you're planning a long trip. Fortunately, Colombia has a wide range of options for phone and internet services that can cater to different budgets and preferences. Here are some of the options you can consider:

1. Local SIM cards: If you have an unlocked phone, you can buy a local SIM card from one of the major carriers in Colombia, such as Claro, Movistar, or Tigo. This will give you a local phone number and access to the carrier's network for calls, texts, and internet services. The prices and plans for local SIM cards vary depending on the carrier and the type of service you need.

2. Roaming: If your phone plan supports international roaming, you can use your phone in Colombia by paying the roaming fees. However, this can be expensive and may not be cost-effective for long-term stays.

3. Wi-Fi hotspots: Most hotels, restaurants, and cafes in Colombia offer free Wi-Fi to their customers. You can also find public Wi-Fi hotspots in major cities such as Bogota, Medellin, and Cartagena. However, be cautious when using public Wi-Fi as they may not be secure and can be vulnerable to cyberattacks.

4. Pocket Wi-Fi devices: If you need constant internet access, you can rent or buy a pocket Wi-Fi device, which can provide internet access for multiple devices simultaneously. These devices can be rented at the airport or in major cities and can be a good option for those traveling in groups.

5. Internet cafes: If you need to use the internet for a short period, you can visit one of the many internet cafes in Colombia. These cafes charge a fee for internet access and may also offer printing and scanning services.

When it comes to phone and internet options, it's important to choose a plan that fits your needs and budget. Before your trip, research the different options and compare the prices and services offered by different providers. Additionally, make sure to check with your phone provider to see if they offer any international plans or discounts for Colombia.

Wi-Fi access and hotspots

In today's digital age, having access to Wi-Fi while traveling is becoming more and more essential. Luckily, Colombia is a country that is well-equipped with Wi-Fi access and hotspots. In this section, we will discuss how to find Wi-Fi access and hotspots in Colombia, as well as some tips for staying connected while on the go.

Most hotels, hostels, and restaurants in Colombia offer free Wi-Fi for customers, so it is easy to stay connected while traveling. Some popular coffee shops like Juan Valdez, OMA, and Tostao also offer free Wi-Fi to customers. Many shopping malls and public places, such as parks and plazas, also provide free Wi-Fi.

If you need to stay connected on the go, you may consider purchasing a local SIM card or a portable Wi-Fi device, also known as a pocket Wi-Fi. You can easily purchase a local SIM card at most phone shops in Colombia. The most popular mobile network operators in Colombia are Claro, Movistar, and Tigo. Before purchasing a SIM card, make sure that your phone is unlocked and compatible with the network you choose.

Portable Wi-Fi devices are also available for rent at airports, hotels, and some travel agencies. These devices allow you to connect multiple devices to Wi-Fi without needing a local SIM card. They are especially useful if you are traveling with a group or need to stay connected on the go.

In addition to Wi-Fi access, Colombia also has a growing number of hotspots, which provide free Wi-Fi in public areas. These hotspots are usually located in parks, plazas, and other public places. Some popular hotspots in Colombia include the Parque de la 93 in Bogotá and the Parque Lleras in Medellín.

It is important to note that while Wi-Fi access and hotspots are widely available in Colombia, internet speeds can vary depending on your location.

In more remote areas or smaller towns, Wi-Fi speeds may be slower or less reliable. In larger cities, however, Wi-Fi speeds are generally fast and reliable.

To stay connected and avoid high data roaming charges, it is recommended that you download offline maps and travel apps before your trip. This way, you can access important information, such as directions, restaurant recommendations, and local events, without needing an internet connection.

In conclusion, staying connected while traveling in Colombia is easy with the widespread availability of Wi-Fi access and hotspots. By following the tips and recommendations in this section, you can stay connected and make the most of your trip to Colombia.

Translation tools and apps

Travelling to a foreign country can be exciting and intimidating at the same time. The language barrier can often pose as a significant obstacle in communication, and that's where translation tools and apps come in handy. In Colombia, Spanish is the official language, and while many people speak English, it is always best to have a translation tool on hand to help navigate the language barrier. Here are some of the best translation tools and apps to consider when traveling to Colombia:

1. Google Translate: Google Translate is a free translation tool that can translate over 100 languages. It's available as a mobile app and a website. With Google Translate, you can translate text, voice, and even images. This app is easy to use, and it's perfect for translating simple phrases and sentences.

2. iTranslate: iTranslate is another popular translation app that can translate over 100 languages. It's available for both iOS and Android devices. In addition to text translations, iTranslate can also translate voice and even entire conversations. It also has a feature that allows you to save your favorite translations for easy access.

3. TripLingo: TripLingo is a travel-specific app that offers translation services, as well as other useful features like a tip calculator, cultural information, and safety tips. The app has a unique feature called

"slang slider," which allows you to adjust the level of formality in your translations based on your audience.

4. Waygo: Waygo is a translation app that specializes in translating Asian languages, including Chinese, Japanese, and Korean. It uses optical character recognition (OCR) technology to translate text in real-time, making it perfect for translating menus and signs.

5. Duolingo: Duolingo is a language-learning app that can help you learn Spanish, which can be useful if you plan on spending an extended period in Colombia. The app is free and offers a gamified approach to learning a new language.

6. Speak & Translate: Speak & Translate is a voice translation app that can translate over 100 languages. It's available for both iOS and Android devices. The app is easy to use, and it can even detect the language being spoken automatically.

When choosing a translation tool or app, consider the features that are most important to you, such as the ability to translate voice or text, real-time translation, or the ability to save favorite translations. It's also a good idea to download the app before your trip and test it out to ensure that it meets your needs. With the right translation tool or app, you can communicate effectively in Colombia and have a more enjoyable trip.

Contacting authorities and embassies

Contacting authorities and embassies is an essential part of travel preparation. Emergencies can happen anytime and anywhere, so it's important to know how to contact local authorities and your embassy in case you need assistance.

First, it's important to know the emergency numbers in Colombia. The emergency number for police, ambulance, and fire services is 123. If you need medical assistance, you can also call the Red Cross at 132.

If you are a foreign national and need assistance, you can contact your embassy in Colombia. Most countries have an embassy or consulate in Bogotá, the capital city. The embassy can provide you with a range of services, including passport renewal, notary services, and emergency assistance.

It's a good idea to have the contact information of your embassy with you at all times. This information is usually available on the embassy's website or through your government's foreign affairs department.

In addition to your embassy, you can also contact the Colombian authorities in case of an emergency. The national police force is known as the Policía Nacional, and they have stations throughout the country. You can also contact the Colombian Ministry of Foreign Affairs for assistance.

It's important to note that the Colombian government may have different procedures and laws than your home country, so it's important to familiarize yourself with local laws and customs before you travel. The embassy can provide you with information on local laws and regulations.

In addition to emergency services and embassies, there are also a number of other organizations that can assist travelers in Colombia. These include the Tourist Assistance Center, which provides information and support to travelers, and the Colombian Tourist Police, who are trained to assist visitors and protect them from crime.

In summary, it's important to be prepared for emergencies and to know how to contact local authorities and your embassy in case you need assistance. Make sure to have the contact information for your embassy with you at all times and familiarize yourself with local laws and customs before you travel. By taking these steps, you can enjoy a safe and enjoyable trip to Colombia.

Staying in touch with family and friends

Staying in touch with family and friends is important for many people when they travel, whether it's to share experiences, ask for advice or simply stay connected with loved ones. Fortunately, there are many ways to stay in touch while traveling in Colombia, from traditional methods like phone calls and postcards to modern technologies like social media and messaging apps.

Here are some tips for staying in touch with family and friends while traveling in Colombia:

1. Phone calls: If you have a mobile phone that is compatible with international networks, you can make phone calls to your family and

friends from anywhere in Colombia. However, keep in mind that international calls can be expensive, so it's a good idea to check with your mobile provider before you leave to see if there are any international calling plans or packages that can help you save money.

2. Messaging apps: Messaging apps like WhatsApp, Facebook Messenger and Telegram are popular in Colombia and can be a great way to stay in touch with family and friends back home. These apps allow you to send text messages, voice messages, photos and videos, and most of them also offer voice and video calling.

3. Social media: Social media platforms like Facebook, Twitter, Instagram and Snapchat are also great for staying in touch with family and friends. You can post updates and photos of your trip, and your loved ones can leave comments and messages to keep in touch.

4. Email: Email is another way to stay in touch with family and friends while traveling. It's a great option if you want to share longer updates and photos, or if you need to send documents or other files.

5. Postcards: Sending postcards is a fun and traditional way to stay in touch with family and friends while traveling. You can find postcards at most tourist shops and post offices, and they usually only cost a few dollars to send.

No matter which method you choose, it's important to remember to stay safe while using technology and to be aware of your surroundings. It's also a good idea to let your loved ones know your travel plans and to check in with them regularly, especially if you're traveling alone or to a remote area. With a little bit of planning and the right tools, you can stay in touch with your family and friends and make the most of your trip to Colombia.

Sustainability and Responsible Travel

Environmental impact and conservation efforts

When traveling to a foreign country, it is essential to be aware of the environmental impact of our actions and take steps to minimize it. Colombia is a country that is blessed with natural resources, and it is our responsibility to conserve and preserve it.

One way to reduce the environmental impact of travel is to pack light and avoid carrying unnecessary items. The more weight we carry, the more fuel is burned, resulting in more pollution. We should also try to use public transportation, walk or cycle whenever possible, rather than hiring a car.

We should also be mindful of our water and electricity usage. Colombia is a country with a hot and humid climate, and we should avoid wasting water, especially when taking showers or brushing our teeth. In addition, we should try to turn off lights, fans, and other electronic devices when not in use.

Conservation efforts are essential for maintaining the biodiversity and ecological balance of Colombia. The country has several national parks, reserves, and protected areas that are home to various endangered species of flora and fauna. We should make an effort to visit these areas and support their conservation efforts through donations or volunteering.

Another way to reduce our environmental impact is to avoid buying single-use plastic items such as water bottles, straws, and bags. Instead, we should carry our reusable water bottles, bags, and utensils. When shopping for souvenirs, we should look for locally made and eco-friendly items.

Finally, we should be mindful of our carbon footprint when flying to Colombia. We can reduce our impact by choosing direct flights instead of connecting flights, opting for economy class rather than first or business class, and offsetting our carbon emissions by supporting a carbon offset program.

In summary, we can make a positive impact on the environment and conservation efforts in Colombia by being mindful of our actions and making conscious decisions to reduce our environmental impact.

Supporting local communities and businesses

Supporting local communities and businesses is an important aspect of responsible and sustainable travel. When travelling to a new destination, it is important to consider the impact of tourism on the local community and to take steps to minimize any negative effects while supporting local initiatives.

One way to support local communities is by staying in locally-owned accommodations such as small guesthouses, bed and breakfasts, or locally-owned hotels. These establishments are often more authentic and offer a more unique experience than large chain hotels. Additionally, the money spent on accommodations goes directly to supporting the local community.

When dining out, look for local restaurants and eateries that use locally sourced ingredients. By supporting local restaurants, you are also supporting local farmers and food producers. Eating locally sourced food can also help to reduce the carbon footprint of your trip, as the food doesn't have to be transported long distances.

Another way to support local communities is by purchasing locally made souvenirs and crafts. Look for local markets and shops that sell handmade goods, and avoid buying mass-produced souvenirs that may be made overseas. By purchasing from local artisans, you are helping to support their livelihoods and preserving local traditions.

Volunteering with local organizations and charities can also be a great way to support the community. Look for opportunities to work with local conservation initiatives, community development projects, or educational programs.

It is also important to be mindful of the environment when travelling. Consider taking public transportation or renting bicycles instead of renting a car. Avoid using single-use plastics such as water bottles, and dispose of waste properly. When hiking or exploring nature, stay on marked trails and avoid damaging natural habitats.

In summary, supporting local communities and businesses is an important aspect of responsible travel. By choosing locally-owned accommodations, dining at local restaurants, purchasing locally-made souvenirs, volunteering with local organizations, and being mindful of the environment, you can help to make a positive impact on the places you visit.

Minimizing waste and carbon footprint

When traveling to Colombia, it's important to be mindful of your environmental impact and try to minimize your waste and carbon footprint. Here are some tips for sustainable travel:

1. Bring a reusable water bottle: Instead of buying single-use plastic water bottles, bring your own refillable bottle. In many cities in Colombia, you can find public water fountains where you can refill your bottle for free.

2. Use public transportation: Taking public transportation, such as buses or trains, is a great way to reduce your carbon footprint. It's also a great way to experience local life and save money.

3. Stay in eco-friendly accommodations: Look for hotels or hostels that have sustainable practices, such as using renewable energy, reducing waste, and conserving water.

4. Bring reusable bags: When shopping or visiting local markets, bring your own reusable bags instead of using plastic bags.

5. Be mindful of your energy use: Turn off lights and electronics when you're not using them, and adjust the temperature in your room to conserve energy.

6. Respect nature and wildlife: When visiting national parks or wildlife areas, follow the rules and regulations, and avoid touching or disturbing the animals or their habitats.

7. Support local conservation efforts: Consider donating to or volunteering with local organizations that work to protect the environment and wildlife in Colombia.

By taking these simple steps, you can help minimize your impact on the environment and support sustainable travel practices in Colombia.

Ethical wildlife tourism practices

Ethical wildlife tourism practices involve respecting the natural habitat and behavior of animals while also ensuring the well-being and safety of both animals and humans. It is important to engage in responsible wildlife tourism to avoid causing harm to wildlife and their habitats. Here are some guidelines for ethical wildlife tourism practices:

1. Do your research: Before booking any wildlife tour, research the operator thoroughly to ensure that they are committed to ethical and sustainable tourism practices. Look for certifications and affiliations with reputable conservation organizations.

2. Avoid wildlife attractions that exploit animals: Avoid activities that involve riding, petting, or posing with captive animals. These types of attractions often involve animal abuse and exploitation, and the animals are kept in poor conditions.

3. Respect animals in their natural habitat: When observing animals in their natural habitat, keep a safe distance and avoid disrupting their natural behavior. Do not feed or touch wildlife, and never disturb nesting or breeding sites.

4. Choose eco-friendly accommodations: Look for accommodations that prioritize sustainability and minimize their environmental impact. Eco-friendly hotels and lodges often have programs in place to reduce waste, conserve energy and water, and support local communities.

5. Follow local rules and regulations: Be aware of local laws and regulations when visiting wildlife areas. Follow all signs and instructions given by park rangers and tour guides.

6. Support local conservation efforts: Visit and support conservation centers and wildlife rehabilitation facilities that are working to protect endangered species and habitats.

7. Be mindful of your waste: Minimize your waste by bringing a reusable water bottle, packing reusable bags for shopping, and avoiding single-use plastics.

By following these guidelines, travelers can engage in ethical wildlife tourism practices and help promote sustainable and responsible tourism.

Responsible volunteering and donation opportunities

Responsible volunteering and donation opportunities can provide a meaningful way for travelers to give back to the communities they visit. However, it is important to choose a responsible and ethical organization that prioritizes sustainable and long-term solutions rather than short-term fixes.

When considering volunteer opportunities, it is important to research the organization and ensure that their practices align with your values. Organizations that prioritize community-driven development and involve local stakeholders in decision-making processes are generally more effective in creating sustainable change. Additionally, it is important to consider the skills and expertise you can offer and whether they align with the needs of the community. For example, if you are a healthcare professional, volunteering at a local clinic may be a more impactful way to give back.

It is also important to approach donations with a similar level of consideration. Rather than donating to large, international organizations, consider supporting local community-based organizations that work directly with the community. These organizations often have a deeper understanding of the local context and are better equipped to create long-term solutions. When donating, ensure that your contribution is transparent and accountable, and that it aligns with the community's needs.

When volunteering or making donations, it is important to consider the potential negative impacts. Voluntourism, where volunteers engage in short-term, unskilled work in developing countries, can often do more harm than good. This is because it perpetuates the cycle of dependency and creates unrealistic expectations for the community. Additionally, donations can sometimes create a reliance on external aid rather than promoting self-sufficiency. To avoid these negative impacts, consider volunteering for longer periods of time and ensure that your skills are well-aligned with the needs of the community. Additionally, work with organizations that prioritize community-driven development and promote self-sufficiency rather than dependence.

In summary, responsible volunteering and donation opportunities can be a meaningful way to give back to the communities you visit. However, it is important to choose an ethical organization that prioritizes sustainable and long-term solutions, and to consider the potential negative impacts of your actions. By taking these factors into account, you can ensure that your contributions make a positive impact on the community.

Pre-departure Checklist

Checklist for travel documents and identification
When planning a trip, it's important to make sure you have all the
necessary travel documents and identification with you. Here's a checklist
of some of the most important documents you should have:

- ✔ Passport: Make sure your passport is valid for at least six months
  from your planned travel dates. Also, ensure that you have enough
  blank pages for visa stamps.

- ✔ Visa: Check if you need a visa to enter the country you plan to visit. If
  you do, make sure you apply for it well in advance.

- ✔ Travel insurance: It's always a good idea to have travel insurance to
  cover unexpected medical expenses, trip cancellations, and other
  travel-related issues.

- ✔ Flight tickets: Make sure you have a copy of your flight itinerary and
  all flight tickets.

- ✔ Hotel reservations: Print out your hotel reservations or have them
  accessible on your phone or tablet.

- ✔ Driver's license: If you plan to drive while on your trip, make sure you
  have your driver's license and an international driving permit if
  required.

- ✔ Credit/debit cards: Take at least two credit/debit cards with you and
  make sure they are valid for use in the country you plan to visit.

- ✔ Health-related documents: Carry any necessary health-related
  documents, such as vaccination certificates or medical prescriptions.

✔ Emergency contact information: Make sure you have the contact information of your embassy or consulate in the country you plan to visit, as well as emergency contact information for your family and friends back home.

✔ Copies of important documents: Take copies of all important documents, including your passport, visa, travel insurance, and credit/debit cards. Keep these copies separate from the originals in case of loss or theft.

By checking off these items on your travel documents and identification checklist, you can help ensure a smooth and stress-free travel experience.

Checklist for health and medical items

Here's a checklist for health and medical items you may need to pack for your trip:

- ✔ Prescription medications: Bring enough medication to last the entire trip, plus a few extra days just in case. Keep the medications in their original packaging with the prescription label on them.

- ✔ Over-the-counter medications: Pain relievers, antihistamines, motion sickness medication, and other remedies for common ailments may come in handy.

- ✔ First-aid kit: Include bandages, antiseptic ointment, gauze, adhesive tape, tweezers, and any other supplies you may need for minor injuries.

- ✔ Insect repellent: Protect yourself from mosquito and other insect bites with a good quality insect repellent.

- ✔ Sunscreen: Protect your skin from the harmful UV rays of the sun by applying a broad-spectrum sunscreen with an SPF of 30 or higher.

- ✔ Personal hygiene items: Bring travel-sized toothbrush, toothpaste, soap, shampoo, and other personal care items.

- ✔ Hand sanitizer: Keep your hands clean and germ-free with a bottle of hand sanitizer.

- ✔ Prescriptions for glasses or contacts: If you wear glasses or contacts, bring a copy of your prescription in case you need to replace them.

- ✔ Travel-sized toilet paper: In case you find yourself in a restroom without toilet paper.

✔ Medical information: Carry information about any medical conditions or allergies you may have, as well as the contact information for your doctor and emergency contacts.

It's always a good idea to check with your doctor or a travel health clinic about any specific health concerns you may have about your destination. They can also advise you on any additional vaccinations or medications you may need.

Checklist for packing essentials

Here's a checklist for packing essentials:

✔ Clothing: Pack clothing according to the weather and the activities you have planned. Include a mix of casual and formal wear. Consider packing light, wrinkle-resistant clothing to minimize the need for ironing.

✔ Footwear: Bring comfortable walking shoes, sandals, and dress shoes for formal events. If you plan to do outdoor activities, pack appropriate footwear such as hiking boots or water shoes.

✔ Toiletries: Toothbrush, toothpaste, deodorant, shampoo, conditioner, soap, razor, and any other personal grooming products you may need. Don't forget to pack sunscreen, insect repellent, and any medications you need.

✔ Electronics: Depending on your needs, you may want to bring a phone, laptop, tablet, camera, or other electronic devices. Don't forget to bring the necessary chargers and adapters.

✔ Travel documents: Don't forget your passport, visa (if required), and any other travel documents. Keep them in a safe and secure place.

✔ Money and credit cards: Bring cash and credit cards for purchases and emergencies. Make sure to notify your bank and credit card company of your travel plans to avoid any issues with transactions.

✔ Travel accessories: Pack a neck pillow, eye mask, earplugs, and a travel blanket to make long flights more comfortable. A travel adapter and a power bank can also come in handy.

✔ Entertainment: Bring a book, magazine, or e-reader to pass the time during long flights or waits at airports. You may also want to pack playing cards or a travel board game for entertainment during downtime.

✔ Baggage: Choose a durable and lightweight suitcase or backpack. Make sure it meets airline size and weight restrictions. Consider packing a foldable bag to use as a daypack or for carrying souvenirs.

✔ Other items: Pack a small first-aid kit, a water bottle, and a reusable shopping bag for carrying groceries or souvenirs. You may also want to bring a small lock to secure your luggage or hostel locker.

Checklist for finances and money management

Here's a checklist for finances and money management when preparing for travel:

- ✔ Check the currency of your destination country and convert your money accordingly.

- ✔ Inform your bank and credit card company about your travel plans to avoid any fraud alerts or account freezing.

- ✔ Carry a mix of cash and credit/debit cards, but don't carry too much cash.

- ✔ Get a travel credit card with no foreign transaction fees, if possible.

- ✔ Keep copies of important documents, such as your passport, travel insurance, and credit cards, in a safe place, and carry extra copies with you.

- ✔ Carry a money belt or travel wallet to keep your cash and cards safe.

- ✔ Use ATMs in safe and crowded areas, and be cautious when withdrawing money.

- ✔ Keep track of your expenses and budget accordingly.

- ✔ If you're traveling for an extended period, consider opening a local bank account.

- ✔ Research the tipping culture of your destination and budget accordingly.

- ✔ Check for duty-free shopping opportunities and tax refunds, if applicable.

✔ Consider purchasing travel insurance to protect yourself against any unexpected expenses.

✔ Make a plan for managing your finances in case of an emergency.

✔ Keep a list of emergency contacts and financial institutions in case of loss or theft of your money or cards.

✔ Finally, be mindful of your spending habits and avoid unnecessary expenses.

Checklist for communication and connectivity

Here's a checklist for communication and connectivity when travelling:

✔ Mobile phone: Bring your mobile phone with you, and make sure it's unlocked so you can use local SIM cards. Consider getting an international plan from your service provider or buying a local SIM card when you arrive.

✔ Chargers and power bank: Don't forget to bring the chargers for your phone, as well as any other electronic devices you're bringing. A power bank is also helpful to have in case you can't find an outlet to charge your devices.

✔ Adapter: Depending on where you're travelling from, you may need an adapter to use your chargers in a different country.

✔ Wi-Fi access: Research where you can find free Wi-Fi hotspots in your destination, such as coffee shops or libraries.

✔ Communication apps: Download communication apps like WhatsApp, Skype, or Viber to make free calls and send messages over Wi-Fi.

✔ Travel apps: Install travel apps like Google Maps, TripAdvisor, and Airbnb to help you navigate and find things to do in your destination.

✔ Language translation app: If you don't speak the local language, download a language translation app like Google Translate to help you communicate with locals.

✔ Emergency contacts: Make sure you have emergency contact information saved on your phone, including the local embassy or consulate, your travel insurance provider, and the local emergency services.

✔ Backup documents: Take photos of important documents like your passport, visa, and travel insurance policy and save them on your phone or in a secure cloud storage app.

✔ Travel journal: Consider bringing a travel journal to record your experiences and keep track of important information like flight times and hotel reservations.

CHAPTER FOUR
During the Trip

Managing travel stress and jet lag

Traveling can be an exciting and rewarding experience, but it can also be stressful and exhausting. Jet lag, in particular, can take a toll on your body and disrupt your travel plans. Here are some tips for managing travel stress and jet lag:

1. Get plenty of rest before your trip. Try to adjust your sleep schedule a few days before you leave to match the time zone of your destination.

2. Stay hydrated. Drink plenty of water before and during your flight to prevent dehydration, which can make jet lag symptoms worse.

3. Move around during your flight. Sitting in one position for a long time can cause stiffness and discomfort. Get up and walk around the cabin or do some simple exercises in your seat to improve circulation.

4. Pack a travel pillow and eye mask. These items can help you get comfortable and get some rest during your flight.

5. Avoid caffeine and alcohol. These can disrupt your sleep and make jet lag symptoms worse.

6. Try to get some sunlight when you arrive at your destination. Exposure to natural light can help reset your body clock and reduce jet lag.

7. Take short naps. If you feel tired during the day, take a short nap to help you feel more refreshed.

8. Use relaxation techniques. Deep breathing, meditation, and other relaxation techniques can help reduce stress and promote relaxation.

9. Take it easy. Don't overdo it with activities and sightseeing right away. Give yourself time to adjust to the new time zone and pace yourself.

By following these tips, you can help manage travel stress and jet lag and enjoy your trip to the fullest.

Tips for staying healthy and safe

Traveling can be exciting, but it can also present health and safety risks. Here are some tips to stay healthy and safe during your trip:

1. Get vaccinated: Before traveling, make sure you are up-to-date on all routine vaccinations and any additional vaccinations recommended for your destination. Consider getting vaccinated against illnesses such as hepatitis A and B, typhoid, yellow fever, and others if recommended by your healthcare provider.

2. Stay hydrated: Dehydration can cause headaches, fatigue, and other symptoms. Make sure to drink plenty of water, especially if you're in a hot climate or doing physical activities.

3. Protect yourself from the sun: Wear sunscreen, protective clothing, and hats to protect your skin from harmful UV rays. Sunburn can lead to skin cancer and other health problems.

4. Wash your hands: Frequent handwashing can help prevent the spread of germs and reduce your risk of getting sick. Use soap and water or hand sanitizer when soap and water are not available.

5. Practice safe food and water habits: Make sure the food you eat is thoroughly cooked, and avoid raw or undercooked foods. Drink only bottled or boiled water, or use a water purification system.

6. Be aware of your surroundings: Keep an eye on your surroundings and avoid dangerous areas. Be aware of the risks associated with crime, terrorism, and natural disasters.

7. Know how to access medical care: Know where to go for medical care if you need it. Make sure you have health insurance that covers medical care while you're abroad.

8. Carry emergency contact information: Make sure you have a list of emergency contacts, including your healthcare provider and insurance company, with you at all times.

9. Practice good sleep habits: Jet lag can disrupt your sleep patterns, leading to fatigue and other symptoms. To minimize the effects of jet lag, try to get plenty of rest before your trip and establish a regular sleep schedule once you arrive.

10. Take breaks and pace yourself: Don't try to do too much too quickly. Take breaks and pace yourself to avoid exhaustion and reduce the risk of injury.

Cultural experiences and activities

When traveling, immersing oneself in the local culture is an important part of the experience. It allows you to learn about the history and traditions of the place you are visiting, as well as gain a deeper understanding of its people and their way of life. Here are some cultural experiences and activities to consider when planning your trip:

A. Visit Museums and Galleries: Museums and galleries are a great way to learn about the local art, history, and culture. In Colombia, there are many museums and galleries worth visiting, such as the Gold Museum in Bogotá, the Botero Museum in Medellín, and the Contemporary Art Museum in Cali. Find all about it below:

BEST MUSEUMS AND GALLERIES

Colombia is a country rich in cultural heritage and has a wealth of museums and galleries that offer visitors the chance to explore its history, art, and architecture. Here are some of the top museums and galleries to visit in Colombia:

1. Gold Museum (Museo del Oro) - Bogotá The Gold Museum in Bogotá is one of the most popular tourist attractions in Colombia. It has an extensive collection of pre-Columbian gold artifacts, which include pottery, jewelry, and textiles. Visitors can also learn about the indigenous peoples who created these objects and their cultural significance.

2. Botero Museum - Bogotá The Botero Museum is named after Colombia's most famous artist, Fernando Botero. It has a large collection of his paintings and sculptures, as well as works by other renowned artists such as Picasso, Renoir, and Dalí.

3. Museum of Antioquia - Medellín The Museum of Antioquia in Medellín houses a vast collection of Colombian art, including works by Fernando Botero, Pedro Nel Gómez, and Débora Arango. It also

has a collection of pre-Columbian objects, as well as colonial and contemporary art.

4. National Museum of Colombia - Bogotá The National Museum of Colombia is one of the oldest and largest museums in the country. It has a vast collection of objects that document Colombia's history and culture, including pre-Columbian art and artifacts, colonial-era paintings and sculptures, and contemporary art.

5. Quinta de Bolívar - Bogotá Quinta de Bolívar is a museum dedicated to the life and legacy of Simón Bolívar, the hero of Colombia's independence. The museum is housed in a historic mansion that was once the residence of the revolutionary leader.

6. Casa Museo Pedro Nel Gómez - Medellín The Casa Museo Pedro Nel Gómez is dedicated to the life and work of the famous Colombian painter Pedro Nel Gómez. It houses a large collection of his paintings and sculptures, as well as works by other Colombian artists.

7. National Museum of Modern Art - Bogotá The National Museum of Modern Art in Bogotá is dedicated to contemporary art from Colombia and around the world. It has a vast collection of paintings, sculptures, installations, and multimedia works.

8. Museo de Arte Contemporáneo de Bogotá (MAC) - Bogotá The Museo de Arte Contemporáneo de Bogotá (MAC) is another museum dedicated to contemporary art. It has a collection of works by Colombian and international artists, as well as a program of temporary exhibitions, performances, and events.

9. Museo de Arte Moderno de Medellín - Medellín The Museo de Arte Moderno de Medellín is a modern and contemporary art museum in Medellín. It has a collection of Colombian and international art, as well as temporary exhibitions, workshops, and events.

10. Casa Museo Francisco José de Caldas - Bogotá The Casa Museo Francisco José de Caldas is dedicated to the life and work of the famous Colombian scientist and philosopher. It is housed in a historic mansion that was once the residence of Caldas, and it includes a collection of his scientific instruments, books, and personal belongings.

These are just a few of the many museums and galleries to visit in Colombia. Each one offers a unique perspective on the country's history, art, and culture, and they are a must-see for anyone interested in learning more about Colombia's rich heritage.

B. Attend Cultural Festivals: Colombia is home to a variety of cultural festivals throughout the year. These festivals celebrate everything from music and dance to food and traditional dress. Some popular festivals include the Barranquilla Carnival, the Medellín Flower Fair, and the Bogotá International Film Festival.

CULTURAL FESTIVALS

Colombia is a country with a vibrant cultural scene, and it hosts numerous cultural festivals throughout the year. These festivals showcase the diversity and richness of Colombian culture, attracting both locals and visitors from around the world. Here are some of the most renowned cultural festivals in Colombia:

1. Carnival of Barranquilla: The Carnival of Barranquilla is one of the largest and most popular carnivals in the world, attracting over one million visitors every year. The carnival takes place in the city of Barranquilla, on the Caribbean coast of Colombia, and it lasts for four days, beginning on the Saturday before Ash Wednesday. The carnival features music, dance, parades, and colorful costumes, and it is recognized as a Masterpiece of the Oral and Intangible Heritage of Humanity by UNESCO.

2. Medellin Flower Fair: The Medellin Flower Fair, also known as Feria de las Flores, is an annual festival that takes place in the city of Medellin. The festival celebrates the diversity and beauty of Colombian flowers, and it features parades, concerts, exhibitions, and other cultural events. The highlight of the festival is the Flower Parade, a colorful procession of floats adorned with flowers.

3. Ibero-American Theater Festival: The Ibero-American Theater Festival is held every two years in the city of Bogota, and it is one of the largest theater festivals in the world. The festival features theater

productions from all over Latin America, Spain, and Portugal, and it attracts thousands of visitors from around the world. The festival also includes workshops, seminars, and other cultural events.

4. Barranquilla International Film Festival: The Barranquilla International Film Festival is an annual event that takes place in the city of Barranquilla. The festival showcases independent films from around the world, with a focus on Latin American cinema. The festival also features workshops, conferences, and other cultural events.

5. Cartagena International Music Festival: The Cartagena International Music Festival is an annual event that takes place in the historic city of Cartagena. The festival features classical music performances by renowned musicians from around the world, as well as other cultural events such as art exhibitions and dance performances.

6. Cali Fair: The Cali Fair, also known as Feria de Cali, is an annual festival that takes place in the city of Cali. The festival celebrates the culture of the Valle del Cauca region, and it features music, dance, bullfighting, and other cultural events. The highlight of the festival is the Salsa Parade, a colorful procession of dancers performing to the rhythm of salsa music.

7. Hay Festival Cartagena: The Hay Festival Cartagena is an annual literary festival that takes place in the city of Cartagena. The festival brings together writers, poets, journalists, and other literary figures from around the world to discuss literature, politics, and culture. The festival also includes book signings, readings, and other cultural events.

These cultural festivals are just a few examples of the rich cultural scene in Colombia. Whether you are interested in music, theater, literature, or dance, there is always something to see and do in Colombia.

C. Try Local Cuisine: Sampling local cuisine is a great way to experience the culture of a place. Colombian cuisine is diverse and delicious, featuring dishes such as empanadas, arepas, and bandeja paisa. Be sure to try the local specialty, ajiaco, a hearty soup made with chicken, potatoes, and corn.

LOCAL CUISINE

Colombia is known for its delicious and diverse cuisine that reflects the country's rich history and cultural influences. From hearty stews to tropical fruits, there is something for everyone to enjoy. Here are some of the most popular dishes and drinks to try while in Colombia:

1. Arepas: Arepas are a staple food in Colombia made from ground maize dough that is shaped into patties and grilled. They can be stuffed with a variety of fillings, including cheese, avocado, and meat.

2. Bandeja Paisa: This is a traditional dish from the Antioquia region of Colombia and is a hearty meal consisting of beans, rice, ground beef, chorizo, fried egg, plantain, and avocado.

3. Empanadas: Empanadas are a popular street food in Colombia made with a crispy corn or wheat dough filled with meat, cheese, or vegetables.

4. Ajiaco: This is a delicious soup made with chicken, potatoes, corn, and guascas, a Colombian herb. It is typically served with avocado and capers.

5. Churrasco: Churrasco is a grilled steak dish typically served with chimichurri sauce, rice, and plantains.

6. Patacones: Patacones are fried plantain slices that are often served as a side dish or snack. They can be topped with cheese, guacamole, or other toppings.

7. Ceviche: Ceviche is a popular seafood dish made with raw fish marinated in citrus juices and served with onions, peppers, and herbs.

8. Lomo Saltado: This dish is a fusion of Chinese and Peruvian cuisine and is popular in Colombia. It is made with stir-fried beef, onions, tomatoes, and french fries, and is typically served with rice.

9. Tamales: Tamales are a traditional dish in Colombia made with corn dough and filled with meat, vegetables, and spices. They are wrapped in banana leaves and steamed.

10.   Coffee: Colombia is known for its high-quality coffee, and you can find it served in cafes and restaurants throughout the country.

In addition to the delicious food, Colombia has some unique drinks to try as well:

1. Aguardiente: This is a popular anise-flavored liquor that is often served as a digestif.

2. Chicha: Chicha is a fermented corn drink that is a traditional beverage in many Latin American countries, including Colombia.

3. Refajo: Refajo is a refreshing drink made with beer, soda, and lime juice.

4. Lulada: Lulada is a sweet and tangy drink made from lulo fruit, a tropical fruit found in Colombia.

5. Limonada de Coco: This is a refreshing drink made with coconut milk, lime juice, and sugar.

Overall, trying the local cuisine and drinks is a must when traveling to Colombia. The country's diverse culinary traditions and flavors are a reflection of its rich cultural history, and trying new foods is a great way to experience the local culture.

D. Learn to Dance: Colombia is known for its vibrant music and dance scene. Take a salsa or cumbia dance lesson to experience the rhythm and energy of these traditional dances.

PLACES TO DANCE AND RELAX
Colombia is known for its lively and vibrant nightlife, with plenty of options for dancing and relaxing. Here are some of the top places to check out:

1. Andres Carne de Res: This restaurant and nightclub located in Bogotá is known for its lively atmosphere and excellent food. It's a great place to go for dinner and drinks before hitting the dance floor.

2. La Fonda Paisa: This traditional restaurant in Medellín is known for its live music and dancing. The atmosphere is lively and fun, and the food is delicious.

3. Café del Mar: This rooftop bar in Cartagena is the perfect place to relax and enjoy a drink while taking in the stunning views of the Caribbean Sea. It's a great spot for a romantic evening or a night out with friends.

4. Theatron: This massive nightclub in Bogotá is one of the largest in Latin America, with multiple dance floors and bars spread out over several levels. It's a great place to dance the night away and experience the local nightlife.

5. Galería Café Libro: This cozy café in Bogotá is a great spot to relax with a book or catch up with friends over coffee. It's known for its eclectic décor and laid-back vibe.

6. La Zona Rosa: This neighborhood in Bogotá is known for its trendy bars, restaurants, and nightclubs. It's a great place to go for a night out on the town and experience the local nightlife.

7. Café Havana: This Cuban-themed bar in Cartagena is known for its live salsa music and lively atmosphere. It's a great place to dance and experience the local music scene.

8. Parque Lleras: This park in the heart of Medellín is surrounded by bars, restaurants, and nightclubs. It's a popular spot for locals and tourists alike, and a great place to experience the local nightlife.

9. El Poblado: This neighborhood in Medellín is known for its upscale restaurants and bars. It's a great place to go for a night out with friends or a romantic evening.

10. Tayrona National Park: If you're looking for a more relaxing experience, head to Tayrona National Park on the Caribbean coast. This beautiful park is home to stunning beaches, hiking trails, and plenty of opportunities for relaxation and rejuvenation.

Overall, Colombia offers plenty of options for both dancing and relaxation, with a lively nightlife scene and beautiful natural landscapes to explore. Whether you're looking for a romantic evening or a night out with friends, there's something for everyone in this vibrant country.

E. Explore Indigenous Communities: Colombia is home to many indigenous communities, each with its own unique culture and traditions. Consider visiting an indigenous community to learn about their way of life and customs.

F. Participate in Eco-Tourism: Colombia has a rich biodiversity and natural beauty that is worth exploring. Consider participating in eco-tourism activities such as hiking, birdwatching, or visiting a nature reserve.

G. Attend a Soccer Game: Soccer is the national sport in Colombia and attending a game is a great way to experience the passion and energy of the local fans.

H. Visit Colonial Towns: Colombia has many charming colonial towns that offer a glimpse into the country's rich history. Some of the most popular colonial towns to visit include Cartagena, Villa de Leyva, and Popayán.

COLONIAL TOWNS

Colombia has a rich colonial heritage, and visitors can explore many towns and cities that have preserved their colonial architecture and traditions. These towns offer a glimpse into Colombia's past and are a perfect destination for history buffs and architecture enthusiasts. Here are some of the most beautiful colonial towns to visit in Colombia:

1. Cartagena: Located on the Caribbean coast, Cartagena is one of Colombia's most popular destinations. The city was founded in 1533 and was an important port for Spanish ships carrying gold and silver back to Europe. The old town is surrounded by a 13-kilometer-long stone wall that was built to protect the city from pirates and other invaders. The old town is full of colonial buildings and narrow streets that are perfect for exploring on foot.

2. Villa de Leyva: Located in the Boyacá department, Villa de Leyva is a well-preserved colonial town that was founded in 1572. The town's main square is one of the largest in South America and is surrounded by colonial buildings and a beautiful church. The town is surrounded by stunning natural landscapes, including the Iguaque National Park.

3. Barichara: Located in the Santander department, Barichara is a charming colonial town that is often referred to as the "most beautiful town in Colombia." The town was founded in 1705 and is known for its cobblestone streets, whitewashed buildings, and red-tiled roofs. Visitors can explore the town's many churches, museums, and galleries, or hike the Camino Real, a historic trail that leads to the nearby town of Guane.

4. Popayán: Located in the Cauca department, Popayán is known as the "white city" for its whitewashed colonial buildings. The city was founded in 1537 and was an important center for colonial trade. Visitors can explore the city's many churches and museums, including the Museum of Religious Art and the Museum of Natural History.

5. Mompox: Located on an island in the Magdalena River, Mompox is a well-preserved colonial town that was founded in 1540. The town's historic center is a UNESCO World Heritage Site and is full of colonial buildings and churches. Visitors can explore the town's many plazas, including the Plaza de la Concepción, which is home to a beautiful colonial church.

These colonial towns offer a glimpse into Colombia's past and are a must-visit for anyone interested in history and architecture.

I. Learn a Local Craft: Colombia is known for its skilled artisans who create beautiful handicrafts such as textiles, ceramics, and jewelry. Consider taking a workshop to learn a local craft and bring home a unique souvenir.

LOCAL CRAFT AND BEST SOUVENIR

Colombia is known for its rich and diverse culture, and its local crafts and souvenirs are a great way to take a piece of it home with you. Here are some of the best souvenir items and local crafts to look out for when in Colombia:

1. Coffee: Colombia is famous for its high-quality coffee, and taking home a bag of freshly roasted beans is a must for any coffee lover.

2. Emeralds: Colombia is one of the largest producers of emeralds in the world, and they can be found in many jewelry stores throughout the country.

3. Woven textiles: Colombia has a long tradition of weaving, and you can find beautiful textiles in many different styles and colors.

4. Handmade pottery: There are many skilled artisans throughout Colombia who make beautiful pottery, from traditional clay pots to more modern designs.

5. Leather goods: Colombia is known for its high-quality leather, and you can find everything from shoes and belts to bags and jackets.

6. Wayuu bags: These colorful, hand-woven bags are made by the indigenous Wayuu people of the Guajira Peninsula.

7. Hammocks: Colombia is a great place to pick up a handmade hammock, perfect for relaxing in the sun.

8. Artisanal chocolates: Colombia has a growing artisanal chocolate industry, and you can find delicious chocolates in many different flavors.

9. Aguardiente: This anise-flavored liquor is a popular drink in Colombia, and makes for a great souvenir or gift.

10. Sombrero vueltiao: This traditional hat, made from woven palm leaves, is a symbol of Colombia and a great souvenir to take home.

When shopping for souvenirs in Colombia, it's important to be aware of counterfeit items, especially when it comes to emeralds and other precious stones. It's best to buy from reputable shops and vendors, and to always ask for a certificate of authenticity.

Additionally, bargaining is common in Colombia, especially in markets and street stalls. Don't be afraid to negotiate on the price, but be respectful and keep in mind that the vendors rely on these sales for their livelihood.

J. Visit Religious Sites: Colombia is a predominantly Catholic country and has many impressive churches and religious sites to visit. The Salt Cathedral in Zipaquirá and the Las Lajas Sanctuary in Ipiales are both popular pilgrimage sites.

BEST RELIGIOUS SITES

Colombia is home to several religious sites, reflecting its diverse religious beliefs and practices. Here are some of the best religious sites to visit in Colombia:

1. Salt Cathedral of Zipaquirá: The Salt Cathedral of Zipaquirá is a Roman Catholic church built inside an abandoned salt mine in Zipaquirá, Cundinamarca. It is one of the most popular religious sites in Colombia and attracts thousands of visitors each year.

2. La Catedral de Sal de Zipaquirá: This cathedral is built entirely of salt blocks and is located in the town of Zipaquirá. It is a unique and impressive work of architecture.

3. Santuario de Las Lajas: This is a basilica church located in Ipiales, Narino, built in Gothic Revival style. It is one of the most visited religious sites in Colombia and is famous for its stunning location, set against the backdrop of a waterfall.

4. Iglesia de San Francisco: The Church of San Francisco is a 16th-century church located in the historic center of Bogotá. It is one of the oldest and most important churches in Colombia, and is a popular pilgrimage site for Catholics.

5. Basílica del Señor de los Milagros de Buga: This is a Roman Catholic basilica located in the city of Buga, Valle del Cauca. It is known for its miraculous image of the Christ of Buga, which is believed to have healing powers.

6. Templo de la Iglesia Adventista del Séptimo Día: The Adventist Church is located in Medellin and is the largest Adventist church in Colombia. It is a beautiful and peaceful place to visit and learn about the Adventist faith.

7. Iglesia de la Veracruz: This is a colonial-era church located in the historic center of Cartagena. It is known for its intricate architecture and beautiful frescoes.

These are just a few of the many religious sites that Colombia has to offer. Whether you are a devout believer or simply interested in exploring different religious traditions, these sites are definitely worth a visit.

Overall, there are many cultural experiences and activities to enjoy in Colombia. By immersing yourself in the local culture, you can gain a deeper appreciation for the country and its people.

Budget management and expense tracking

Budget management and expense tracking are essential aspects of travel planning. Proper management of your finances can help you to stay within your budget and avoid overspending. Here are some tips for managing your travel expenses:

1. Create a travel budget: Before you start planning your trip, create a budget for all of your expenses, including airfare, accommodations, transportation, meals, and activities. Be realistic and take into account any unexpected expenses that may arise.

2. Research prices: Research the prices of flights, accommodations, and other travel expenses before making any bookings. This will give you a good idea of how much you should expect to spend.

3. Use travel rewards: If you have travel rewards credit cards or loyalty programs, use them to help offset the cost of your trip. You may also be able to earn additional rewards points or miles by booking certain activities or tours.

4. Book in advance: Booking your accommodations, activities, and transportation in advance can often save you money. Many hotels and airlines offer discounted rates for early bookings.

5. Use public transportation: Using public transportation, such as buses or trains, is often much cheaper than taking taxis or renting a car. Plus, it can be a great way to explore the local culture and get a feel for the city.

6. Eat like a local: Eating at local restaurants or markets can often be much cheaper than eating at touristy restaurants. Plus, you'll get a taste of the local cuisine.

7. Keep track of your expenses: Use a travel expense tracker to keep track of all of your expenses. This will help you stay within your budget and avoid overspending.

8. Be prepared for emergencies: Have a backup plan in case of unexpected expenses, such as medical emergencies or lost luggage. Consider purchasing travel insurance to cover any unforeseen costs.

By following these tips, you can effectively manage your travel expenses and ensure that you stay within your budget while still having a great trip.

Staying connected with loved ones

Staying connected with loved ones while traveling is important to many people. Fortunately, technology has made it easier than ever to stay in touch with family and friends from anywhere in the world. Here are some tips for staying connected while traveling:

1. Use social media: Social media platforms like Facebook, Twitter, and Instagram allow you to share updates, photos, and videos with your friends and family in real-time. You can also use private messaging features to chat with individuals or groups.

2. Video chat: Video chat apps like Skype, Zoom, and FaceTime allow you to see and speak with your loved ones face-to-face, no matter where you are in the world. This can be especially helpful for keeping in touch with young children or elderly family members.

3. Send postcards or letters: Sometimes the old-fashioned way is the best way. Sending postcards or letters to loved ones is a thoughtful way to let them know you're thinking of them, and can be a fun way to document your travels.

4. Use messaging apps: Messaging apps like WhatsApp, Viber, and Line are popular for staying in touch with friends and family while traveling. These apps allow you to send text messages, photos, and videos over Wi-Fi or cellular data.

5. Make a phone call: Sometimes a simple phone call is all you need to catch up with loved ones. If you have an international plan on your phone, you can make calls from anywhere in the world. Alternatively, you can use a local SIM card or purchase a prepaid phone card.

6. Schedule regular check-ins: Set a regular time to check in with loved ones, whether it's daily, weekly, or monthly. This can give you both something to look forward to and help you stay connected, even if you're in different time zones.

Overall, staying connected with loved ones while traveling is important for maintaining relationships and can make your trip more enjoyable. By using a combination of technology and old-fashioned communication methods, you can stay in touch with those who matter most.

Returning Home

Adjusting to normal life after travel

Adjusting to normal life after travel can be a challenge for many people, especially if the trip was long or if you experienced significant cultural differences. Here are some tips for making the transition back to everyday life a little smoother:

1. Give yourself time: Don't expect to feel completely back to normal immediately after returning home. It can take a few days or even weeks to readjust, so be patient with yourself.

2. Maintain your routine: Try to get back into your normal routine as soon as possible, including eating meals at regular times, sleeping on a regular schedule, and exercising regularly.

3. Stay in touch: Keep in touch with the people you met while traveling, and share your experiences with your friends and family back home. This can help you process your experiences and feel more connected to the world.

4. Incorporate what you learned: Think about the new skills, perspectives, and insights you gained from your travels, and try to incorporate them into your daily life. This can help you maintain a sense of connection to the places and people you encountered on your trip.

5. Practice self-care: Travel can be exhausting, both physically and emotionally. Make sure to take care of yourself by eating healthy foods, getting enough sleep, and engaging in activities that bring you joy and relaxation.

6. Plan your next trip: Having something to look forward to can help ease the transition back to normal life. Start planning your next trip, even if it's just a short weekend getaway.

Remember, everyone's experience with travel is unique, and it's okay to take your time readjusting to normal life. By giving yourself time, staying in touch with loved ones, and taking care of yourself, you can make the transition back to everyday life as smooth as possible.

Tips for reflecting on the trip

Traveling can be a life-changing experience, and it's important to take time to reflect on your trip once you return home. Here are some tips for reflecting on your trip:

1. Write in a journal: Keeping a travel journal is a great way to remember your trip and process your thoughts and emotions. Take some time each day to write down what you did, how you felt, and what you learned.

2. Look through your photos: Going through your photos can help you remember the sights, sounds, and experiences of your trip. Take some time to sort through your photos and create a photo album or scrapbook.

3. Share your experiences with others: Talk to your friends and family about your trip and share your experiences. You can also write a blog post or create a video to share your journey with others.

4. Plan your next adventure: Planning your next trip can help you stay excited and motivated. Take some time to research your next destination and start planning your itinerary.

5. Incorporate what you learned into your daily life: Traveling can teach us a lot about ourselves and the world around us. Think about what you learned on your trip and how you can apply those lessons to your daily life.

By taking the time to reflect on your trip, you can gain a deeper understanding of yourself and the world around you.

Sharing experiences with others

Sharing experiences with others after a trip can be an exciting and rewarding experience. It allows you to relive your adventures, share what you've learned, and inspire others to explore new places. Here are some tips for sharing your travel experiences with others:

1. Create a blog or social media account: If you want to share your experiences with a wider audience, consider creating a blog or social media account dedicated to your travels. This allows you to share photos, stories, and tips with others who are interested in travel.

2. Host a slideshow or presentation: Invite friends and family over for a slideshow or presentation of your trip. This is a great way to share your experiences in a more personal and interactive way.

3. Keep a travel journal: Keeping a travel journal during your trip allows you to capture your thoughts and experiences in real-time. You can use this as a reference when sharing your experiences with others.

4. Print photos and create a scrapbook: Printing out your favorite photos and creating a scrapbook is a fun and creative way to document your trip. You can also use this as a visual aid when sharing your experiences with others.

5. Attend travel meetups or events: Attend travel meetups or events in your area to meet other travelers and share your experiences. This is a great way to connect with like-minded individuals and learn about new destinations.

6. Share your experiences with your community: Consider sharing your experiences with your local community by volunteering to give a talk at a local school or community center. This is a great way to inspire others to travel and learn about different cultures.

Remember, sharing your travel experiences with others is a great way to relive your adventures, inspire others, and create a sense of community among travelers.

Evaluating the success of the preparation process

Evaluating the success of the preparation process is an important step towards ensuring a successful trip. It allows travelers to assess their level of readiness and identify areas that need improvement in future travels. Here are some tips for evaluating the success of the preparation process:

1. Review the travel checklist: A travel checklist is a handy tool that can help travelers stay organized and ensure that they don't forget anything important. After the trip, review the checklist to see if there were any items that were not used, and if there were any items that were missing.

2. Assess the quality of travel documents and identification: Check whether all travel documents and identification were in order and up-to-date. Were there any issues at immigration or customs that could have been avoided by better preparation?

3. Evaluate budget management and expense tracking: Were you able to stick to your budget during the trip? Did you track your expenses effectively? If not, identify the areas where you overspent and see how you can improve in the future.

4. Assess communication and connectivity: Were you able to stay connected with loved ones during the trip? Were there any issues with internet connectivity or communication that could have been avoided by better preparation?

5. Reflect on cultural experiences and activities: Did you have the opportunity to participate in local cultural experiences and activities? If not, identify the reasons why and see how you can improve in the future.

6. Evaluate your health and safety during the trip: Were you able to stay healthy and safe during the trip? Did you take any unnecessary risks that could have been avoided? If so, identify the reasons why and see how you can improve in the future.

7. Assess the impact of the trip on the environment and local communities: Did you take steps to minimize your environmental impact and support local communities during the trip? If not, identify

the areas where you could have done better and see how you can improve in the future.

8. Reflect on the overall experience: Finally, reflect on the overall experience of the trip. Were you satisfied with the itinerary and activities? Did you learn anything new? What would you do differently in the future?

By evaluating the success of the preparation process, travelers can learn from their experiences and improve their future travels.

Planning for future trips

Planning for future trips can be an exciting experience, especially after a successful trip. Here are some tips for planning future trips:

1. Decide on the destination: Start by deciding on the destination you would like to visit next. Consider factors such as your interests, budget, time available, and travel goals.

2. Research the destination: Once you have decided on a destination, research it thoroughly to learn more about the culture, climate, local customs, attractions, and activities.

3. Create a budget: Determine how much you can afford to spend on the trip, and create a budget that includes all expenses such as airfare, accommodation, transportation, food, and activities.

4. Choose the best time to travel: Consider the weather conditions, peak season, and off-peak season for your destination. Choose a time that is convenient for you and fits your budget.

5. Book your flights and accommodation: Book your flights and accommodation in advance to avoid last-minute price hikes and availability issues.

6. Plan your itinerary: Create an itinerary that includes all the places you would like to visit and activities you would like to do. Allow for some flexibility in case you need to make changes.

7. Check for travel advisories: Check for any travel advisories or restrictions for your destination, especially if you are traveling internationally.

8. Get travel insurance: Consider purchasing travel insurance to protect yourself in case of any unforeseen events such as flight cancellations or medical emergencies.

9. Prepare your travel documents: Ensure that your passport and other travel documents are up-to-date and valid for your travel dates.

10. Pack wisely: Pack light and bring only the essential items that you will need. Consider the climate and local customs when choosing your clothing and accessories.

Remember to always stay safe and informed during your travels. Happy planning!

CHAPTER FIVE

Traveling With

Traveling with Children

Preparing children for travel

Preparing children for travel can be an exciting and rewarding experience, but it can also be a bit stressful if you're not adequately prepared. Here are some tips for preparing children for travel:

1. Involve them in the planning process: Including children in the planning process can help them feel more invested in the trip and give them a sense of ownership over the experience.

2. Talk about the destination: Discussing the destination with your children can help build excitement and anticipation. You can share pictures, videos, and stories about the place you will be visiting.

3. Practice packing: Give your children the opportunity to practice packing their own bags. This can help them feel more independent and responsible.

4. Discuss cultural differences: Depending on where you're traveling, there may be cultural differences that your children need to be aware of. Talk to them about any customs, beliefs, or practices they should be aware of.

5. Discuss safety: Talk to your children about staying safe while traveling. This includes discussing things like stranger danger, staying together in crowded areas, and being aware of their surroundings.

6. Bring familiar items: Bringing along familiar items from home, like a favorite toy or stuffed animal, can help children feel more comfortable and secure while traveling.

7. Plan for downtime: Traveling can be tiring, especially for children. Make sure to plan for downtime, like naps or quiet activities, so everyone can recharge.

8. Consider a travel journal: A travel journal can be a fun way for children to document their experiences and remember the trip. You can provide them with a notebook, stickers, and other supplies to help them create their own journal.

9. Have fun: Most importantly, remember to have fun! Traveling with children can be challenging at times, but it's also a great opportunity to make memories and have new experiences together.

Selecting family-friendly destinations and accommodations

Traveling with children can be an incredibly rewarding experience, but it also requires a bit of extra planning to ensure everyone is comfortable and happy throughout the trip. Colombia is a great destination for families with children, as there are plenty of family-friendly destinations and accommodations to choose from. In this guide, we will discuss how to select family-friendly destinations and accommodations in Colombia.

Destinations for Families with Children

When it comes to selecting destinations for families with children, there are a few things to keep in mind. First and foremost, you'll want to choose destinations that offer plenty of activities and attractions that are suitable for children. You'll also want to consider the safety of the destination, as well as the ease of getting around.

Here are some family-friendly destinations to consider when traveling to Colombia:

- Cartagena: This historic city on the Caribbean coast is a great destination for families with children. The walled city offers plenty of attractions, including museums, parks, and beaches. The nearby Rosario Islands are also a popular destination for families.

- Bogota: Colombia's capital city has plenty of family-friendly attractions, including parks, museums, and cultural sites. The Maloka Interactive Center is a great destination for children, as it offers interactive exhibits on science and technology.

- Medellin: Known as the "City of Eternal Spring," Medellin offers a mild climate and plenty of family-friendly attractions. The Parque Explora is a great destination for children, as it features an aquarium, a planetarium, and plenty of interactive exhibits.

- Santa Marta: This coastal city is a great destination for families who enjoy outdoor activities. The nearby Tayrona National Park offers plenty of opportunities for hiking and swimming, and the Lost City trek is a great adventure for older children.

Accommodations for Families with Children

When it comes to selecting accommodations for families with children, you'll want to look for properties that offer plenty of space and amenities. You'll also want to consider the location of the property, as well as the safety and security of the area.

Here are some types of accommodations to consider when traveling with children:

- Vacation Rentals: Vacation rentals offer plenty of space and privacy, which can be ideal for families with children. Look for properties that offer plenty of amenities, such as a fully equipped kitchen, a washer and dryer, and a swimming pool.

- Family-Friendly Hotels: Many hotels offer family-friendly amenities, such as swimming pools, playgrounds, and children's activities. Look for properties that offer connecting rooms or suites, as well as cribs or rollaway beds.

- All-Inclusive Resorts: All-inclusive resorts can be a great option for families, as they offer plenty of activities and amenities in one location. Look for properties that offer children's clubs or activities, as well as all-inclusive meal plans.

- Hostels: Hostels can be a budget-friendly option for families with children. Look for properties that offer private rooms or family rooms, as well as common areas where children can socialize with other travelers.

Tips for Traveling with Children

Here are a few tips to keep in mind when traveling with children in Colombia:

- Pack plenty of snacks and drinks: Children can get hungry and thirsty while traveling, so be sure to pack plenty of snacks and drinks to keep them satisfied.

- Plan for downtime: Traveling can be tiring for children, so be sure to plan for plenty of downtime where they can rest and relax.

- Bring entertainment: Long car rides or flights can be boring for children, so be sure to bring plenty of entertainment, such as books, games, and movies.

- Be prepared for the weather: Colombia's climate can vary depending on the region, so be sure to pack appropriate clothing and gear for the weather conditions. For example, if you're traveling to the coast, you'll want to pack plenty of sunscreen, hats, and swimsuits, while if you're traveling to the mountains, you'll want to pack warm clothing and jackets.

- Practice safety precautions: Colombia is generally a safe destination, but it's always a good idea to practice safety precautions, such as keeping a close eye on your children in crowded areas and avoiding walking alone at night.

- Learn some Spanish: While many Colombians speak English, it's always a good idea to learn some basic Spanish phrases, especially if you're traveling with children. Knowing some Spanish can be helpful in communicating with locals and navigating unfamiliar areas.

In conclusion, traveling with children can be a fun and rewarding experience, especially when visiting family-friendly destinations in Colombia. When selecting destinations and accommodations, consider the safety, activities, and amenities available for children. Remember to pack appropriately, plan for downtime, and practice safety precautions while traveling. With a little bit of planning and preparation, your family trip to Colombia is sure to be a success.

Tips for returning home and adjusting to normal life

Traveling with children can be an exciting and memorable experience, but the return home can sometimes be a challenging adjustment. Here are some tips to help you and your children ease back into normal life after a trip to Colombia.

- Give yourself and your children time to adjust: It's important to remember that traveling can be tiring, especially for children. When you return home, give yourselves a few days to rest and adjust to the time difference and the demands of daily life. Avoid scheduling any major activities or appointments immediately upon your return.

- Keep your travel memories alive: Encourage your children to talk about their favorite memories from the trip and share your own experiences. You can create a photo album, scrapbook or video to keep these memories alive and revisit them whenever you want.

- Re-establish routines: Children thrive on routine, so try to re-establish your daily routines as quickly as possible. This includes meal times, bedtimes, and school or work schedules. It may take some time for your children to get back into their routines, but stick with it and be consistent.

- Get back to healthy habits: Traveling can sometimes disrupt healthy habits like regular exercise and healthy eating. When you return home, try to get back to these habits as quickly as possible. Encourage your children to eat healthy meals and snacks and engage in regular physical activity.

- Plan some fun activities: To help ease the transition back to normal life, plan some fun activities for you and your children. This could be something as simple as a trip to the park or a movie night at home. Having something to look forward to can make the return home less daunting.

- Stay connected: If you met locals or made new friends while traveling, stay connected with them. You can exchange emails, social media contacts, or even plan to visit again. This can help your children remember their experience and maintain an interest in the world around them.

- Talk to your children about the experience: Encourage your children to talk about their experience in Colombia. This will give them a chance to process their emotions and reflect on what they learned. You can also use this opportunity to talk about the cultural differences they observed and the importance of respecting other cultures.

In conclusion, traveling with children can be a wonderful experience that creates lasting memories. However, returning home can sometimes be challenging. By giving yourself and your children time to adjust, re-establishing routines, and staying connected with your travel experiences, you can make the transition back to normal life a little easier.

Traveling with Disabilities

Identifying accessible destinations and accommodations
Traveling with disabilities can present unique challenges, but it shouldn't stop you from exploring and enjoying new destinations. Colombia offers a wide range of accessible destinations and accommodations for travelers with disabilities. Here are some tips on how to identify accessible destinations and accommodations in Colombia:

- Research destination accessibility: Research the accessibility of your desired destinations before you go. Look for information on accessible transportation, attractions, and accommodations. You can also contact local tourist offices or travel agencies to inquire about accessibility.

- Look for accessible accommodations: Look for hotels, resorts, or vacation rentals that offer accessible rooms and facilities. Make sure to inquire about accessibility features such as wheelchair ramps, grab bars, and accessible bathrooms.

- Use accessible transportation: Use accessible transportation such as taxis or buses equipped with wheelchair lifts or ramps. Consider renting an accessible vehicle if necessary.

- Plan for accessible activities: Plan for accessible activities such as visiting museums or attractions with accessible entrances and exhibits. Look for accessible tours or guided experiences that cater to travelers with disabilities.

- Consider hiring a travel agent: Consider hiring a travel agent who specializes in accessible travel to help plan your trip. They can provide valuable insights and recommendations on accessible destinations and accommodations.

- Ask for assistance: Don't be afraid to ask for assistance when traveling. Many hotels, restaurants, and attractions are willing to provide additional assistance to travelers with disabilities. It's also a good idea to inform the airline or transportation provider in advance of any special needs.

- Use technology: Use technology to your advantage by downloading apps or using websites that offer information on accessible destinations and accommodations. Apps like AccessNow and Wheelmap can help identify accessible places and facilities.

In conclusion, identifying accessible destinations and accommodations in Colombia is an important aspect of traveling with disabilities. By researching destination accessibility, looking for accessible accommodations, using accessible transportation, planning for accessible activities, considering hiring a travel agent, asking for assistance, and using technology, you can help ensure a safe and enjoyable trip to Colombia.

Planning for transportation and mobility

When traveling with disabilities, planning for transportation and mobility is essential to ensure a safe and enjoyable trip. In Colombia, there are several transportation options available for travelers with disabilities. Here are some tips on how to plan for transportation and mobility when traveling with disabilities in Colombia:

- Research transportation options: Research the transportation options available in the area you will be visiting. Look for accessible public transportation options such as buses or trains with wheelchair ramps or lifts.

- Consider hiring a private driver: Consider hiring a private driver who specializes in accessible transportation. They can provide a comfortable and convenient way to get around, especially if you need assistance with mobility.

- Rent an accessible vehicle: Renting an accessible vehicle can be a great option for travelers with disabilities who want more freedom and independence. Make sure to research accessible vehicle rental companies in advance and book your vehicle early.

- Use ride-sharing services: Many ride-sharing services in Colombia offer accessible vehicles or have partnerships with accessible transportation providers. Consider using these services to get around during your trip.

- Plan for airport transportation: Plan for airport transportation in advance. Many airports offer accessible transportation options such as wheelchair assistance or accessible shuttle services.

- Request assistance: Don't be afraid to request assistance when traveling. Many transportation providers, such as airlines, offer assistance for travelers with disabilities. Make sure to request assistance in advance and inform the provider of your specific needs.

- Bring mobility aids: If you use a mobility aid such as a wheelchair or walker, make sure to bring it with you on your trip. Research the accessibility of your destinations and accommodations to ensure they can accommodate your specific mobility needs.

In conclusion, planning for transportation and mobility is essential when traveling with disabilities in Colombia. By researching transportation options, considering hiring a private driver, renting an accessible vehicle, using ride-sharing services, planning for airport transportation, requesting assistance, and bringing mobility aids, you can help ensure a safe and enjoyable trip to Colombia.

Managing medical and health needs

Managing medical and health needs is a crucial aspect of traveling with disabilities. Here are some tips on how to manage your medical and health needs when traveling in Colombia:

- Consult with your doctor: Before traveling, consult with your doctor to ensure that you are fit to travel. Ask for advice on managing your medical needs during your trip.

- Pack sufficient medication: Make sure to pack sufficient medication for the entire trip, plus extra in case of unexpected delays. Keep your medication in your carry-on luggage to ensure that it is easily accessible.

- Carry a medical ID card: Carry a medical ID card with you at all times that contains information about your medical condition, allergies, and emergency contacts. This will ensure that you can receive the appropriate medical care in case of an emergency.

- Research medical facilities: Research the medical facilities available in the areas you will be visiting. Look for hospitals and clinics that are equipped to handle your specific medical needs.

- Inform your travel companions: Inform your travel companions about your medical needs and how they can assist you in case of an emergency.

- Consider travel insurance: Consider purchasing travel insurance that covers your medical needs. Make sure to read the policy carefully to ensure that it covers all of your specific medical needs.

- Plan for accessibility: Plan for accessibility when it comes to medical facilities. Make sure that the facilities you will be visiting are accessible and equipped to handle your specific medical needs.

In conclusion, managing medical and health needs is crucial when traveling with disabilities in Colombia. By consulting with your doctor, packing sufficient medication, carrying a medical ID card, researching medical facilities, informing your travel companions, considering travel insurance, and planning for accessibility, you can help ensure a safe and enjoyable trip to Colombia.

Coping with disability-related challenges during travel

Traveling with a disability can present challenges, but with the right planning and preparation, you can overcome these challenges and enjoy your trip. Here are some tips on coping with disability-related challenges during travel in Colombia:

- Stay positive: A positive attitude can go a long way in coping with disability-related challenges. Focus on the things that you can do and enjoy, rather than on the things that you can't do.

- Be prepared: Plan for the unexpected by bringing extra medication, mobility aids, and other essential items. Research accessibility information for your destinations and accommodations in advance.

- Ask for assistance: Don't be afraid to ask for assistance when you need it. Many people are willing to help, but they may not know how to assist you unless you ask.

- Advocate for yourself: Advocate for your needs and rights as a person with a disability. If you encounter any accessibility issues or discrimination during your trip, speak up and advocate for yourself.

- Take breaks: Traveling can be exhausting, especially if you have a disability. Take breaks and rest when you need to, and don't push yourself too hard.

- Connect with local disability organizations: Connecting with local disability organizations can provide you with valuable resources and support. They can also offer advice on accessible attractions and activities in the area.

- Stay informed: Stay informed about your rights as a person with a disability when traveling in Colombia. Research the laws and regulations that protect people with disabilities, and know how to file a complaint if necessary.

In conclusion, coping with disability-related challenges during travel in Colombia requires a combination of preparation, advocacy, and self-care. By staying positive, being prepared, asking for assistance, advocating for yourself, taking breaks, connecting with local disability organizations, and staying informed, you can overcome the challenges and enjoy your trip to Colombia.

Advocating for disability rights and accommodations

Advocating for disability rights and accommodations is important for ensuring that people with disabilities are able to fully participate in society and enjoy equal access to opportunities. Here are some ways that you can advocate for disability rights and accommodations in Colombia:

- Get involved with disability rights organizations: There are many disability rights organizations in Colombia that work to promote the rights of people with disabilities. Consider getting involved with one of these organizations, volunteering your time or supporting them financially.

- Speak out about accessibility issues: If you encounter accessibility issues during your travels, speak out about them. Contact the relevant authorities or organizations and let them know about the issue. Share your experiences on social media to raise awareness and encourage change.

- Use your voice: As a person with a disability, your voice is important. Use your voice to advocate for yourself and others. Speak up about the issues that matter to you and encourage others to do the same.

- Educate others: Educate others about disability rights and accommodations. Share information about the barriers that people with disabilities face and the importance of accessibility. Encourage others to become advocates for disability rights and accommodations.

- Support disability-inclusive policies and practices: Support policies and practices that promote disability inclusion and accessibility. Vote for politicians who prioritize disability rights and accommodations, and support businesses and organizations that are committed to accessibility.

- Celebrate disability diversity: Celebrate the diversity of people with disabilities and their contributions to society. Challenge stereotypes and misconceptions about disability, and promote a positive image of disability.

In conclusion, advocating for disability rights and accommodations in Colombia requires a combination of individual and collective action. By getting involved with disability rights organizations, speaking out about accessibility issues, using your voice, educating others, supporting disability-inclusive policies and practices, and celebrating disability diversity, you can help promote equality and inclusion for people with disabilities in Colombia.

Traveling Solo

Safety considerations for solo travel

Traveling solo can be a rewarding and empowering experience, but it also requires extra attention to safety considerations. Here are some tips to help ensure a safe solo travel experience in Colombia:

- Research your destination: Before you travel, research your destination thoroughly. Learn about the local customs, laws, and safety issues, as well as any areas to avoid.

- Stay in safe accommodations: Choose safe and reputable accommodations, such as hotels or hostels with good reviews. Consider staying in well-lit areas and avoid secluded or dimly lit streets.

- Keep your itinerary private: Avoid sharing your travel itinerary or plans with strangers, especially on social media. This can help reduce the risk of becoming a target for theft or other crimes.

- Stay alert and aware of your surroundings: Be vigilant and aware of your surroundings at all times. Avoid getting distracted by your phone or other devices, and trust your instincts if you feel uncomfortable or threatened.

- Avoid excessive drinking: Drinking excessively can impair your judgment and make you more vulnerable to crime. Be mindful of your alcohol consumption and avoid walking alone late at night.

- Use transportation safely: Use only reputable transportation services, such as licensed taxis or ride-sharing services. Avoid getting into unmarked vehicles or accepting rides from strangers.

- Keep your valuables safe: Keep your valuables, such as your passport, cash, and electronics, secure and out of sight. Consider using a money belt or other discreet means of carrying important items.

- Stay connected: Keep in touch with family and friends and let them know your travel plans and itinerary. Check in regularly with them, especially if you plan to explore off-the-beaten-path destinations.

In conclusion, solo travel can be a safe and rewarding experience if you take the necessary precautions. By researching your destination, staying in safe accommodations, keeping your itinerary private, staying alert, avoiding excessive drinking, using transportation safely, keeping your valuables secure, and staying connected, you can help ensure a safe and enjoyable solo travel experience in Colombia.

Coping with loneliness and social isolation

Traveling solo can be an amazing adventure, but it can also be challenging when it comes to coping with loneliness and social isolation. Here are some tips to help you cope with loneliness and stay connected while traveling solo in Colombia:

- Meet locals and other travelers: One of the best ways to combat loneliness is to meet new people. Consider joining a local tour, attending events, or using social apps designed for meeting other travelers. You can also try staying in a hostel, which is a great way to meet people from all over the world.

- Stay connected with family and friends: Even though you are traveling solo, it's important to stay connected with your loved ones. Use technology to stay in touch with family and friends through video chats, messaging apps, and social media.

- Engage in activities that interest you: Traveling solo gives you the freedom to engage in activities that you love. Whether it's exploring museums, hiking, or taking a cooking class, do things that you are passionate about. You are more likely to meet like-minded people and make new friends.

- Journaling: Writing in a journal can be a great way to reflect on your experiences and process your emotions. It's also a great way to keep track of all the amazing things you've done during your travels.

- Be open to new experiences: One of the joys of solo travel is the ability to be spontaneous and try new things. Be open to new experiences, and you may find yourself making new friends and having the time of your life.

- Take care of yourself: Traveling can be stressful, so it's important to take care of yourself. Make sure to eat well, get enough sleep, and exercise regularly. These things will help you feel better and more energized, which can help combat feelings of loneliness.

In conclusion, traveling solo can be a great opportunity to grow and explore, but it can also be challenging when it comes to loneliness and social isolation. By meeting locals and other travelers, staying connected with family and friends, engaging in activities that interest you, journaling, being open to new experiences, and taking care of yourself, you can help combat loneliness and have an amazing solo travel experience in Colombia.

Tips for making connections and meeting people

Traveling solo can be a great opportunity for personal growth and adventure, but it can also be lonely at times. If you're looking to make connections and meet people while traveling solo, here are some tips to get you started:

- Stay in social accommodations: Hostels, Airbnb rentals, and guesthouses are great places to stay if you're traveling solo and looking to meet people. These accommodations often have communal areas where travelers can hang out and socialize.

- Join group activities: Many destinations offer group activities like walking tours, food tours, and adventure activities. These are great opportunities to meet other travelers who share similar interests.

- Attend social events: Check out local events like concerts, festivals, and community gatherings. These events offer a great opportunity to meet locals and other travelers.

- Use social media: Use social media platforms like Facebook, Instagram, and Twitter to connect with other travelers who are also in the area. You can also use apps like Meetup and Couchsurfing to connect with like-minded travelers.

- Volunteer: Volunteering can be a great way to meet people and give back to the community. Look for local volunteer opportunities through organizations like VolunteerMatch and HelpX.

- Take classes: Sign up for a language class, cooking class, or dance class. This is a great way to learn something new while also meeting people who share your interests.

- Be open-minded and approachable: When traveling solo, it's important to be open-minded and approachable. Smile, say hello, and strike up a conversation with fellow travelers or locals.

- Learn some of the local language: Learning a few phrases in the local language can go a long way in making connections with locals. It shows that you're making an effort to connect with the culture and can make people more willing to engage with you.

- Be safe: While it's important to be open and approachable, it's also important to stay safe. Always trust your instincts and be cautious when meeting new people. Stick to public places and let someone know where you're going.

In conclusion, traveling solo can be an amazing experience that allows you to meet new people and have unique adventures. By staying in social accommodations, joining group activities, attending social events, using social media, volunteering, taking classes, being open-minded and approachable, learning the local language, and being safe, you can make the most of your solo travel experience and connect with people along the way.

Managing logistics and decision-making

Traveling solo can be liberating, but it can also be challenging to manage all the logistics and decision-making on your own. Here are some tips to help you manage logistics and make decisions when traveling solo:

- Plan ahead: Before you leave for your trip, research your destination and plan your itinerary. This will help you make informed decisions when you're on the road.

- Use a travel app: There are many travel apps available that can help you manage logistics like transportation, accommodations, and activities. These apps can also provide recommendations and reviews from other travelers.

- Be flexible: While it's important to have a plan, it's also important to be flexible. Unexpected situations can arise, and being open to change can make your solo travel experience more enjoyable.

- Prioritize your safety: When traveling solo, it's important to prioritize your safety. Make sure you have copies of important documents like your passport and travel insurance, and keep them in a safe place. Stay in safe accommodations and avoid walking alone at night in unfamiliar areas.

- Ask for advice: Don't be afraid to ask for advice from locals, other travelers, or travel professionals. They can provide valuable insights and recommendations that can make your trip more enjoyable.

- Trust your instincts: As a solo traveler, you'll need to rely on your instincts to make decisions. If something doesn't feel right, trust your gut and make a different decision.

- Take breaks: Traveling solo can be exhausting, both physically and mentally. Take breaks when you need them and give yourself time to rest and recharge.

- Practice self-care: Traveling solo can also be emotionally challenging. Practice self-care by meditating, journaling, or doing activities that bring you joy.

In conclusion, traveling solo can be a rewarding experience, but it requires careful planning and decision-making. By planning ahead, using travel apps, being flexible, prioritizing safety, asking for advice, trusting your instincts, taking breaks, and practicing self-care, you can manage the logistics and decision-making involved in solo travel and make the most of your trip.

Reflecting on the experience of solo travel

Traveling solo can be a transformative experience that allows you to grow and learn about yourself in new ways. Here are some tips for reflecting on your solo travel experience:

- Take time to reflect: After your trip, take some time to reflect on your experiences. Consider what you learned, what you enjoyed, and what you would do differently in the future.

- Write in a journal: Writing in a journal can help you process your thoughts and emotions from your trip. Consider writing about your experiences, what you learned, and how you grew during your trip.

- Share your experiences: Talk to friends and family about your solo travel experience. Sharing your experiences with others can help you gain new perspectives and insights.

- Stay in touch with people you met: If you met people during your trip, stay in touch with them. This can help you maintain connections and gain new insights into the places you visited.

- Use your experience to set goals: Consider using your solo travel experience to set new goals for yourself. Perhaps you discovered a new passion or realized that you want to make changes in your life. Use these insights to set goals for the future.

- Look at your photos: Looking at your photos from your trip can help you remember your experiences and reflect on your journey.

- Consider your next solo adventure: If you enjoyed your solo travel experience, consider planning your next adventure. Use what you learned from your previous trip to plan your next journey.

In conclusion, solo travel can be a transformative experience that allows you to grow and learn about yourself. By taking time to reflect, writing in a journal, sharing your experiences, staying in touch with people you met, using your experience to set goals, looking at your photos, and planning your next solo adventure, you can continue to grow and learn from your experiences.

Traveling for Business

Managing work and travel schedules

Traveling for business can be a rewarding and exciting experience, but it also requires careful planning and management of work and travel schedules. Here are some tips to help you manage your work and travel schedules when traveling for business:

- Plan ahead: Before you leave for your trip, create a detailed itinerary that includes your work commitments, travel arrangements, and downtime. Make sure you have all the information you need for your business meetings, such as the location, time, and agenda.

- Use a travel app: There are many travel apps available that can help you manage your travel schedule, including booking flights and accommodations, tracking expenses, and keeping track of your itinerary.

- Prioritize your work commitments: When traveling for business, your work commitments should be your top priority. Make sure you have enough time to prepare for your meetings, attend them, and follow up on any action items.

- Use downtime effectively: When you have downtime during your trip, use it effectively. Catch up on work, explore the local area, or simply relax and recharge.

- Stay organized: Keep all your travel documents, work materials, and other important items in one place. This will help you stay organized and avoid losing important items.

- Communicate with your team: Keep in touch with your team back at the office to make sure everything is running smoothly while you're away. Make sure they know how to contact you in case of an emergency.

- Be flexible: Unexpected situations can arise when traveling for business, so it's important to be flexible. Stay calm and adapt to changes as needed.

- Take care of yourself: Business travel can be stressful, so it's important to take care of yourself. Make sure you get enough sleep, eat well, and exercise regularly.

In conclusion, managing work and travel schedules when traveling for business requires careful planning and organization. By planning ahead, using a travel app, prioritizing your work commitments, using downtime effectively, staying organized, communicating with your team, being flexible, and taking care of yourself, you can make the most of your business travel experience.

Selecting appropriate accommodations and transportation

If you are traveling to Colombia for business, selecting appropriate accommodations and transportation is crucial for a successful trip. Here are some tips to help you choose the right accommodations and transportation for your business trip to Colombia:

Accommodations:

- Consider the location: Choose a hotel that is close to your business meetings or conference venue. In Colombia, major cities such as Bogota, Medellin, and Cartagena have plenty of hotel options located in or near business districts.

- Check for amenities: Look for hotels that offer amenities such as high-speed internet, meeting rooms, and a fitness center. These can make your business trip more productive and comfortable.

- Read reviews: Check online reviews to get an idea of the quality and service of different hotels. This can help you avoid unpleasant surprises during your stay.

- Consider safety: Colombia has a history of safety concerns, so it's important to choose a hotel located in a safe area. Look for hotels that have good security measures in place.

Transportation:

- Use reputable taxi companies: When traveling around Colombia, it's important to use reputable taxi companies to ensure your safety. Use apps like Cabify or Uber to book your rides.

- Consider hiring a driver: If you prefer to have a more personal and reliable mode of transportation, consider hiring a driver. Your hotel can usually recommend reputable drivers or car services.

- Check for public transportation: In major cities such as Bogota and Medellin, there is a reliable public transportation system. Consider using the Transmilenio bus system in Bogota or the Metro system in Medellin.

- Consider safety: When choosing transportation, consider safety as a top priority. Avoid taking risks, especially if you are traveling in an unfamiliar area.

In conclusion, selecting appropriate accommodations and transportation is crucial when traveling to Colombia for business. By considering location, amenities, reviews, safety, and transportation options, you can choose the right accommodations and transportation for your business trip to Colombia.

Maintaining productivity and focus during travel

Maintaining productivity and focus during travel is crucial when traveling to Colombia for business. Here are some tips to help you stay productive and focused during your trip:

- Plan ahead: Plan your schedule and agenda in advance to make the most of your time in Colombia. Use tools such as Google Calendar or Trello to organize your itinerary and keep track of your appointments.

- Stay connected: Make sure you have a reliable internet connection and all the necessary equipment such as a laptop or smartphone to stay connected and work remotely if needed.

- Take breaks: While it's important to stay productive, it's also important to take breaks and recharge. Take breaks to explore the local culture or take a walk to clear your mind.

- Manage jet lag: Jet lag can negatively impact your productivity and focus. To minimize jet lag, try to adjust your sleep schedule a few days before your trip, stay hydrated, and take naps if necessary.

- Stay organized: Keep your important documents such as passports, travel documents, and business cards in one place to avoid losing them. Use tools such as Evernote or OneNote to keep track of your notes and ideas.

- Use downtime effectively: Use downtime during your trip, such as waiting at the airport or during transportation, to catch up on work or emails.

- Stay healthy: Staying healthy is important for maintaining productivity and focus. Make sure to eat healthy meals, stay hydrated, and get enough sleep.

In conclusion, maintaining productivity and focus during travel is crucial when traveling to Colombia for business. By planning ahead, staying connected, taking breaks, managing jet lag, staying organized, using downtime effectively, and staying healthy, you can make the most of your business trip to Colombia.

Managing expenses and finances

Managing expenses and finances is an important aspect of any business trip, including when traveling to Colombia for business. Here are some tips to help you manage your expenses and finances during your trip:

- Create a budget: Before your trip, create a budget that includes all expenses such as transportation, accommodations, meals, and incidentals. Stick to your budget as much as possible to avoid overspending.

- Use credit cards: Use credit cards instead of cash whenever possible. This makes it easier to track your expenses and provides additional protection against fraud.

- Keep receipts: Keep all receipts for expenses incurred during your trip. This includes receipts for meals, transportation, and accommodations. This will make it easier to track your expenses and file reimbursement requests.

- Use expense management software: Consider using an expense management software such as Expensify or Concur to track your expenses and submit reimbursement requests.

- Ask for receipts in Spanish: If possible, ask for receipts in Spanish. This will help avoid confusion and make it easier to track expenses.

- Consider currency exchange rates: When exchanging currency, be aware of the current exchange rates. Use online tools such as XE.com to check current exchange rates.

- Keep track of exchange fees: When using credit cards or withdrawing cash from ATMs, keep track of exchange fees. These fees can add up quickly and impact your budget.

- Communicate with your employer: If you have any questions or concerns about your expenses or finances, communicate with your employer or travel manager. They can provide guidance and help ensure your expenses are in compliance with company policies.

In conclusion, managing expenses and finances is important when traveling to Colombia for business. By creating a budget, using credit cards, keeping receipts, using expense management software, considering currency exchange rates, keeping track of exchange fees, and communicating with your employer, you can effectively manage your expenses and finances during your trip.

Balancing work and personal time during travel

When traveling to Colombia for business, it's important to find a balance between work and personal time to make the most of your trip. Here are some tips to help you balance work and personal time during your trip:

- Schedule personal time: Set aside time in your schedule to explore the local culture and attractions. Research the top sights and activities in the area and plan ahead to make the most of your personal time.

- Involve colleagues: If possible, involve your colleagues in your personal activities. This can help build relationships and create a more relaxed and enjoyable environment.

- Use weekends or downtime: If you have weekends or downtime during your trip, use this time to explore the area and enjoy personal activities. Plan ahead to make the most of your time and make sure to communicate your plans with your employer or travel manager.

- Use technology: Use technology such as Skype or FaceTime to stay in touch with family and friends back home. This can help you stay connected and maintain a healthy work-life balance.

- Prioritize rest: It's important to prioritize rest and relaxation during your trip. Make sure to get enough sleep and take breaks throughout the day to recharge and stay focused.

- Be flexible: Be flexible and willing to adjust your schedule as needed. Unexpected opportunities may arise, and it's important to take advantage of these opportunities to make the most of your trip.

In conclusion, balancing work and personal time during travel is important when traveling to Colombia for business. By scheduling personal time, involving colleagues, using weekends or downtime, using technology, prioritizing rest, and being flexible, you can find a balance between work and personal time and make the most of your trip.

Traveling for Study Abroad

Preparing for academic and cultural challenges

When traveling for a study abroad program, it's important to prepare for both academic and cultural challenges that you may face. Here are some tips to help you prepare for these challenges:

- Research the academic expectations: Research the academic expectations and requirements of the program you will be attending. Familiarize yourself with the curriculum, grading system, and academic standards to ensure you are adequately prepared.

- Communicate with professors and advisors: Communicate with your professors and advisors before your trip to ensure you understand their expectations and requirements. This can help you prepare for coursework and exams and ensure a smooth transition into the academic environment.

- Learn about the local culture: Learn as much as possible about the local culture before your trip. Research customs, traditions, and social norms to better understand the local community and avoid cultural misunderstandings.

- Practice the local language: If the program is in a foreign language, practice the language before your trip. This can help you communicate more effectively with locals and navigate the academic environment.

- Be open-minded: Be open-minded and willing to adapt to new cultural experiences. Embrace new customs and traditions, and try to see things from a different perspective.

- Seek out support resources: Seek out support resources such as international student services, academic advisors, and peer mentors. These resources can provide guidance and support throughout your academic and cultural transition.

- Prepare for homesickness: Prepare for homesickness by staying in touch with family and friends back home, and by finding ways to stay connected to your home culture while abroad.

In conclusion, traveling for a study abroad program can be both academically and culturally challenging. By researching academic expectations, communicating with professors and advisors, learning about the local culture, practicing the local language, being open-minded, seeking out support resources, and preparing for homesickness, you can better prepare for the challenges and make the most of your study abroad experience.

Selecting appropriate study abroad programs and accommodations

When planning to travel for a study abroad program, selecting appropriate study abroad programs and accommodations is crucial. Here are some tips to help you select the best program and accommodations for your study abroad experience:

- Research different programs: Research different study abroad programs to find one that fits your academic and personal goals. Consider factors such as location, academic offerings, program duration, and cost.

- Consider program accreditation: Consider choosing a study abroad program that is accredited by a reputable organization. Accredited programs typically ensure high-quality academic offerings and provide support services for students.

- Look for on-site support: Look for study abroad programs that offer on-site support services such as local staff, peer mentors, and housing assistance. Having support available can make the transition to a new country easier and help you navigate any challenges that may arise.

- Consider housing options: Consider your housing options when selecting a study abroad program. Options may include living with a host family, in a residence hall, or in an apartment. Choose an option that suits your needs and preferences.

- Check program reviews: Check program reviews and ratings from other students who have participated in the program. This can provide valuable insight into the program's strengths and weaknesses.

- Plan for cost: Plan for the cost of the study abroad program and accommodations. Look for scholarships, grants, and other funding opportunities to help offset the cost.

- Communicate with your home institution: Communicate with your home institution to ensure that the study abroad program and accommodations meet the academic requirements for your degree program.

In conclusion, selecting appropriate study abroad programs and accommodations is critical to having a successful study abroad experience. By researching different programs, considering accreditation and support services, looking at housing options, checking program reviews, planning for cost, and communicating with your home institution, you can find the best program and accommodations for your needs and goals.

Managing academic and travel schedules

Traveling to study abroad can be both exciting and challenging, especially when it comes to managing academic and travel schedules. Here are some tips to help you manage both:

- Plan ahead: Plan ahead to ensure you have enough time to manage both academic and travel schedules. Create a detailed itinerary for your travel and academic schedule, including important dates and deadlines.

- Use technology: Use technology to help you stay organized and manage your schedule. Use a calendar app to keep track of your schedule, set reminders, and sync your schedule across all your devices.

- Communicate with professors: Communicate with your professors to ensure they are aware of your travel plans and any potential conflicts with your academic schedule. Be proactive in communicating with them about any accommodations you may need, such as completing assignments or exams remotely.

- Prioritize academic work: Prioritize your academic work to ensure you are meeting the expectations of the program. Make sure you are allocating enough time for studying and completing assignments, while also allowing time for travel and exploration.

- Manage your time wisely: Manage your time wisely to ensure you are making the most of your academic and travel experiences. Use downtime during travel to catch up on reading or studying, and try to balance your academic workload with your travel schedule.

- Be flexible: Be flexible and willing to adapt your travel plans to accommodate your academic schedule. Consider alternative travel plans that can accommodate academic obligations.

- Seek support when needed: Seek support from your program's academic advisors or international student services if you are struggling to manage your academic and travel schedules. They can provide guidance and support to help you balance both.

In conclusion, managing academic and travel schedules while studying abroad can be challenging. By planning ahead, using technology, communicating with professors, prioritizing academic work, managing your time wisely, being flexible, and seeking support when needed, you can effectively manage both and make the most of your study abroad experience.

Adapting to cultural differences and language barriers

Traveling to study abroad can be a unique opportunity to experience a new culture and immerse yourself in a different way of life. However, adapting to cultural differences and language barriers can also be a challenging aspect of studying abroad. Here are some tips to help you adapt to cultural differences and overcome language barriers:

- Research the culture: Before you travel, research the culture of the country you will be studying in. Learn about the local customs, values, and beliefs. This can help you understand the cultural differences you may encounter and adapt more easily.

- Learn the language: Try to learn at least some basic phrases in the local language to help you communicate with locals. Consider taking language classes or using language learning apps to improve your language skills.

- Be open-minded: Be open-minded and willing to learn about new customs and ways of life. Embrace the differences and try to understand why they exist.

- Observe and learn: Observe the locals and how they interact with each other. Learn from their behavior and use it as a guide to navigate your own interactions.

- Ask for help: Don't be afraid to ask for help from locals or other international students who may have already adapted to the cultural differences.

- Join cultural events: Join cultural events and activities organized by your program or the local community. This can help you immerse yourself in the local culture and make connections with locals.

- Be respectful: Show respect for the local culture and customs. Be mindful of your behavior and try to avoid any actions that may be considered offensive.

In conclusion, adapting to cultural differences and language barriers while studying abroad can be challenging, but it can also be a rewarding experience. By researching the culture, learning the language, being open-minded, observing and learning, asking for help, joining cultural events, and being respectful, you can successfully adapt to the cultural differences and make the most of your study abroad experience.

Reflecting on the study abroad experience

Reflecting on your study abroad experience can help you gain a deeper understanding of yourself, the world around you, and the impact that studying abroad has had on your personal and academic growth. Here are some tips for reflecting on your study abroad experience:

- Keep a journal: Consider keeping a journal to document your experiences, thoughts, and feelings throughout your study abroad program. This can help you reflect on your experiences and see how you've grown and changed over time.

- Share your experience: Share your experience with others, whether it's with friends and family back home or with other students who may be considering studying abroad. This can help you solidify your own thoughts and feelings about your experience and also help others who may be interested in studying abroad.

- Think about what you learned: Think about what you learned academically, personally, and culturally while studying abroad. Consider how your experience has impacted your future goals and aspirations.

- Consider challenges and growth opportunities: Reflect on the challenges you faced during your study abroad experience and how you overcame them. Also, consider the growth opportunities that arose from those challenges and how they have impacted your personal and academic growth.

- Stay in touch with your study abroad program: Stay in touch with your study abroad program, whether it's through alumni events or social media groups. This can help you continue to feel connected to the program and maintain the friendships and connections you made while studying abroad.

Overall, reflecting on your study abroad experience can help you gain a better understanding of yourself and the world around you. By keeping a journal, sharing your experience, thinking about what you learned, considering challenges and growth opportunities, and staying in touch with your study abroad program, you can gain a deeper appreciation for the impact that studying abroad has had on your personal and academic growth.

Traveling for Volunteer Work

Identifying appropriate volunteer opportunities and organizations

If you're interested in traveling for volunteer work, it's important to identify appropriate volunteer opportunities and organizations to ensure that your time, resources, and efforts are being used effectively and ethically. Here are some tips for identifying appropriate volunteer opportunities and organizations:

- Research the organization: Before committing to a volunteer opportunity, research the organization thoroughly. Look for information about their mission, values, and goals, as well as their track record and reputation. Check for any red flags, such as a lack of transparency, questionable practices, or negative reviews from past volunteers.

- Consider your skills and interests: Consider your skills and interests when choosing a volunteer opportunity. Look for opportunities that align with your personal and professional goals, and where you can use your skills and expertise to make a meaningful contribution.

- Evaluate the impact: Consider the impact of the volunteer work you'll be doing. Look for organizations that have a clear understanding of the needs of the community they serve and have a sustainable and long-term approach to addressing those needs. Make sure that the volunteer work you'll be doing is meaningful and has a positive impact on the community.

- Look for support and resources: Look for organizations that provide support and resources to their volunteers, such as training, orientation, and supervision. This can help ensure that you're able to make the most of your volunteer experience and that your work is effective and impactful.

- Check for ethical practices: Look for organizations that adhere to ethical practices and values. This includes being transparent about their finances and operations, respecting the rights and dignity of the community they serve, and avoiding any activities that may cause harm.

By following these tips, you can identify appropriate volunteer opportunities and organizations that align with your values and goals, and where you can make a meaningful contribution while also having a positive impact on the community you serve.

Preparing for cultural and logistical challenges

Preparing for cultural and logistical challenges is an important aspect of traveling for volunteer work. Here are some tips to help you prepare:

- Research the local culture: Before you travel, research the local culture and customs of the community you'll be working with. This can help you understand and respect cultural differences, avoid cultural misunderstandings, and build meaningful relationships with the people you'll be working with.

- Learn the local language: If the community you'll be working with speaks a language other than your own, consider learning some basic phrases and vocabulary before you travel. This can help you communicate with the people you'll be working with and show that you're making an effort to understand and respect their culture.

- Prepare for logistical challenges: Volunteer work often involves working in remote or under-resourced areas, which can present logistical challenges such as limited access to transportation, electricity, and running water. Research the area you'll be traveling to and prepare accordingly. Consider packing essential items like a first aid kit, insect repellent, and a water filter or purification tablets.

- Be open-minded and flexible: Volunteer work can be unpredictable, and you may encounter unexpected challenges or situations. Be open-minded and flexible, and be willing to adapt to changing circumstances. This can help you stay positive and focused on your goals, and make the most of your volunteer experience.

- Build a support network: Building a support network can be helpful in navigating cultural and logistical challenges. This could include other volunteers, local staff members, or community members. Take the time to build relationships with the people you'll be working with, and be willing to ask for help and support when you need it.

By preparing for cultural and logistical challenges before you travel, you can help ensure that you're able to navigate any obstacles that may arise during your volunteer work. This can help you have a more meaningful and impactful experience, and make a positive difference in the community you serve.

Managing travel and accommodation logistics

If you're traveling to Colombia for volunteer work, managing travel and accommodation logistics is an important part of ensuring a successful trip. Here are some tips to help you with this:

- Research transportation options: Depending on where you'll be volunteering, you may need to research transportation options in advance. Colombia has a wide range of transportation options, including buses, taxis, and domestic flights. Depending on the location of your volunteer work, you may need to book transportation in advance or arrange for a private driver.

- Consider accommodation options: There are a variety of accommodation options available in Colombia, including hotels, hostels, and Airbnb rentals. Depending on your budget and preferences, you may want to research different options in advance and book your accommodations before you travel. Some volunteer organizations may also offer housing options for volunteers.

- Plan for safety and security: Colombia has made significant progress in improving safety and security in recent years, but it's still important to take precautions. Before you travel, research safety tips and advice for the specific areas you'll be visiting. This may include avoiding certain neighborhoods or taking precautions like using a money belt or carrying a photocopy of your passport.

- Pack appropriately: Depending on the nature of your volunteer work, you may need to pack specific items like work gloves, sturdy shoes, or insect repellent. Be sure to research the weather and climate in the area you'll be visiting, and pack accordingly.

- Stay in touch with your volunteer organization: Your volunteer organization can be a valuable resource for managing travel and accommodation logistics. Be sure to stay in touch with them and ask for advice or assistance if you encounter any challenges or need help with booking transportation or accommodations.

By taking the time to research transportation and accommodation options, plan for safety and security, and stay in touch with your volunteer organization, you can help ensure a smooth and successful trip to Colombia for volunteer work.

Balancing volunteer work with personal travel time

When traveling to Colombia for volunteer work, it's important to balance your volunteer work with personal travel time. Here are some tips to help you manage this:

- Plan your schedule in advance: Before you leave for Colombia, create a schedule that outlines your volunteer work commitments as well as any personal travel plans you may have. This will help you prioritize your time and ensure that you have enough time to accomplish both.

- Take advantage of weekends and free time: Depending on your volunteer schedule, you may have weekends or free time during the week. Use this time to explore Colombia and visit nearby attractions.

- Involve your volunteer organization: Your volunteer organization may be able to help you plan personal travel time. Ask for their advice and recommendations on places to visit or activities to do during your free time.

- Be flexible: While it's important to have a plan, it's also important to be flexible. Unexpected opportunities may arise during your volunteer work or personal travel time, so be open to changing your plans if needed.

- Take care of yourself: Balancing volunteer work with personal travel time can be tiring. Be sure to take care of yourself by getting enough rest, eating well, and staying hydrated.

By planning your schedule in advance, taking advantage of free time, involving your volunteer organization, being flexible, and taking care of yourself, you can balance your volunteer work with personal travel time during your trip to Colombia.

Reflecting on the volunteer work experience

Volunteering in Colombia can be a rewarding and fulfilling experience. Here are some tips for reflecting on your volunteer work experience:

- Keep a journal: During your volunteer work, keep a journal to record your experiences and thoughts. Write about what you did each day, how you felt, and what you learned. Reflect on your goals for volunteering and whether or not you achieved them.

- Talk to other volunteers: Talk to other volunteers about their experiences and what they have learned. Share your own experiences and thoughts. You may gain new insights or perspectives that you hadn't considered before.

- Stay in touch with the organization: After you return home, stay in touch with the organization you volunteered with. Share your thoughts and feedback about the experience. Ask how you can continue to support the organization from afar.

- Incorporate what you learned into your daily life: Think about how the volunteer work experience has changed you. Are there new habits or perspectives you want to incorporate into your daily life? Make a plan for how you will do this.

- Consider volunteering again: If you had a positive experience volunteering in Colombia, consider volunteering again in the future. This could be with the same organization or a different one. Reflect on what you learned and how you can continue to grow as a volunteer.

By keeping a journal, talking to other volunteers, staying in touch with the organization, incorporating what you learned into your daily life, and considering volunteering again, you can reflect on and learn from your volunteer work experience in Colombia.

Conclusion

Final tips and advice for successful travel

Congratulations on planning your trip to Colombia! Here are some final tips and advice for a successful travel experience:

- Be prepared: Do your research and plan ahead. Make sure you have all the necessary documents, vaccinations, and travel insurance.

- Be open-minded: Colombia is a diverse country with a rich culture and history. Be open to new experiences and try new things.

- Be respectful: Show respect for the local culture, customs, and people. Learn some basic Spanish phrases and use them when interacting with locals.

- Stay safe: Colombia has come a long way in terms of safety, but it's still important to be cautious. Avoid areas with high crime rates and take precautions such as not carrying around large amounts of cash or valuable items.

- Have fun: Colombia is a beautiful country with a lot to offer. Enjoy the food, music, art, and natural beauty. Take time to relax and enjoy your surroundings.

- Stay flexible: Travel plans can change unexpectedly, so be prepared to be flexible and adapt to new situations.

By being prepared, open-minded, respectful, safe, and flexible, you can have a successful and enjoyable travel experience in Colombia. Safe travels!

Resources for further information and assistance

If you need more information and assistance in planning your trip to Colombia, there are several resources available to you:

- Colombia's official tourism website, ProColombia, provides comprehensive information on travel destinations, activities, and events in Colombia.

- The U.S. Department of State's website offers information on travel advisories and safety tips for Americans traveling to Colombia.

- Lonely Planet's Colombia travel guidebook is a great resource for trip planning, with information on transportation, accommodations, and popular tourist attractions.

- The Colombia Travel Blog provides helpful tips and advice for travelers to Colombia, with detailed information on specific regions and cities.

- Travel forums like TripAdvisor and Reddit's r/travel community can also be helpful resources for asking questions and getting advice from other travelers who have visited Colombia.

Finally, consider reaching out to a travel agency or tour operator specializing in Colombia travel for personalized assistance in planning your trip.

By using these resources and reaching out to experts, you can feel confident in your travel preparations and have a successful trip to Colombia.

Glossary of travel-related terms and concepts.

Here is a glossary of travel-related terms and concepts:

- Accommodation: a place where travelers can stay overnight, such as a hotel, hostel, guesthouse, or vacation rental.

- Backpacking: a style of travel that involves traveling with only a backpack, staying in budget accommodations, and relying on public transportation or walking.

- Budget travel: traveling on a tight budget, often staying in hostels or budget accommodations and eating cheaply.

- Cultural immersion: experiencing and learning about the local culture and customs of a destination through activities such as food tours, language classes, and cultural events.

- Ecotourism: tourism that focuses on responsible travel and sustainable practices, often involving visits to natural areas or wildlife reserves.

- Itinerary: a detailed plan of travel that includes destinations, activities, and transportation.

- Jet lag: a temporary sleep disorder caused by crossing multiple time zones quickly, resulting in fatigue, insomnia, and other symptoms.

- Local experience: traveling like a local and experiencing a destination's culture and way of life, often through homestays or tours led by locals.

- Passport: a government-issued document that serves as identification and allows travel between countries.

- Responsible tourism: a type of travel that aims to minimize the negative impacts of tourism on the environment and local communities, often involving sustainable practices and supporting local businesses.

- Solo travel: traveling alone, often for personal growth or to meet new people.

- Tourist visa: a document issued by a country's government allowing a traveler to enter and stay in the country for a specific period of time.

- Voluntourism: combining volunteer work with travel, often involving service projects such as teaching or conservation work.

- Wanderlust: a strong desire to travel and explore the world.

- Adventure travel: a type of travel that involves outdoor activities such as hiking, camping, and adventure sports.

- Cultural tourism: tourism that involves visiting historical or cultural sites, museums, and attending cultural events.

- All-inclusive: a travel package that includes meals, accommodations, and activities for a flat fee.

- Baggage allowance: the maximum weight and number of bags allowed on a flight or other transportation.

- Car rental: renting a vehicle for personal transportation while traveling.

- Exchange rate: the value of one currency in relation to another.

- Frequent flyer program: a loyalty program offered by airlines that rewards customers for their travel with points or miles that can be redeemed for free flights, upgrades, or other benefits.

- Guidebook: a travel book that provides information on destinations, accommodations, and activities.

- Homestay: staying with a local family in their home, often organized through a homestay program.

- Insurance: protection against financial loss due to unforeseen events such as illness, injury, or trip cancellation.

- Local cuisine: the traditional or popular food of a destination, often a highlight of culinary tourism.

- Passport validity: the length of time a passport is valid for international travel, often at least six months from the date of entry.

- Tour operator: a company that creates and sells travel packages or tours, often including transportation, accommodations, and activities.

- Travel advisory: a warning or alert issued by a government or travel organization regarding safety or security risks in a specific destination.

- Visa requirements: the documentation and procedures required for entering a country, often including a visa application and fees.

.

By familiarizing yourself with these travel-related terms and concepts, you can be better prepared and informed for your next travel experience.

BONUS ITINERARIES

Colombia is a diverse and beautiful country with many amazing destinations to explore. Here are three great itineraries to consider for your trip to Colombia:

- The Andes Mountains and Coffee Region:

This itinerary focuses on the stunning mountainous region of Colombia and the famous coffee plantations. Start in Bogotá, the capital city, and explore its museums, historic sites, and vibrant nightlife. Next, head to the colonial town of Villa de Leyva, known for its well-preserved architecture and picturesque plaza. From there, travel to the Coffee Region, where you can stay on a coffee plantation and learn about the production process. Take a tour of the coffee farms and explore the charming towns of Salento and Filandia. Finish your trip in the city of Medellín, famous for its innovative transportation system, cultural events, and thriving nightlife.

- Caribbean Coast and Cartagena:

This itinerary focuses on Colombia's stunning Caribbean coast and the historic city of Cartagena. Start in the vibrant city of Barranquilla, known for its lively Carnival celebrations. Next, head to Santa Marta, a colonial city with a beautiful beach and access to Tayrona National Park. Spend some time exploring the park's lush jungle and pristine beaches before heading to Cartagena. This colonial gem is known for its colorful buildings, historic forts, and delicious seafood. Take a walking tour of the old town, relax on the beaches of nearby islands, and explore the local markets and restaurants.

- Amazon Rainforest and Leticia:

This itinerary focuses on Colombia's wild and remote Amazon rainforest region. Start in the city of Bogotá and then fly to the southern city of Leticia.

From there, take a boat trip to explore the wildlife-rich Amazon River and the dense jungle. Go on a guided hike to discover exotic plants and animals, including monkeys, sloths, and colorful birds. Spend some time with indigenous communities and learn about their traditional way of life. At night, take a guided canoe trip to see the nocturnal animals and listen to the sounds of the jungle. This itinerary offers an unforgettable adventure for nature lovers and adventure seekers.

No matter which itinerary you choose, Colombia offers a wealth of unique and exciting experiences. With its friendly people, beautiful landscapes, and rich culture, Colombia is a perfect destination for your next adventure.

Printed in Great Britain
by Amazon

40192833R00089